MEN OF STYLE

For Pelham and Renwick, my
Men of Style

Josh Sims

MEN OF STYLE

LAURENCE KING PUBLISHING

CONTENTS

6   INTRODUCTION

8   GIANNI AGNELLI
12   FRED ASTAIRE
18   CHET BAKER
22   CECIL BEATON
26   GEORGE BEST
30   DAVID BOWIE
34   MICHAEL CAINE
38   TRUMAN CAPOTE
42   JOHNNY CASH
46   WINSTON CHURCHILL
50   GARY COOPER
54   GABRIELE D'ANNUNZIO
58   MILES DAVIS
64   SAMMY DAVIS JR
68   JAMES DEAN
72   ALAIN DELON
76   JOHNNY DEPP
80   DUKE OF WINDSOR
86   DOUGLAS FAIRBANKS JR
90   WALT FRAZIER
94   SERGE GAINSBOURG
98   CARY GRANT
104   JIMI HENDRIX
108   DAVID HOCKNEY
112   JOHN F. KENNEDY
116   JACK KEROUAC
120   JEAN RENÉ LACOSTE
124   RALPH LAUREN
128   BOB MARLEY
132   MARCELLO MASTROIANNI
136   STEVE MCQUEEN
140   JIM MORRISON
144   PAUL NEWMAN
148   TOMMY NUTTER
152   PABLO PICASSO
156   ELVIS PRESLEY
160   ROBERT REDFORD
164   KEITH RICHARDS
168   FRANK SINATRA
174   MARK TWAIN
178   ANDY WARHOL
182   ORSON WELLES
186   OSCAR WILDE

190   PICTURE CREDITS/
       ACKNOWLEDGEMENTS

There are many men of style. Most are not famous – you see them up and down the streets. 'Street style', as a category of photography, has been predicated on their existence. But what draws the eye to them? For one, it is not an appreciation for fashion. Following fashion is easy – a fact that has excluded many possible candidates from this book. Dressing with a personal style is something altogether harder – it requires an appreciation for form, colour, texture and composition; an artist's perspective, if you like, applied to whatever one picks out of one's wardrobe each morning, quite possibly at a time when thinking clearly about the triviality of what to wear is not high on the day's agenda.

Dressing with a personal style may not result in a look that is in any way radical – certainly, to buck convention too hard is, arguably, to buck that definition of style laid down by Coco Chanel as being something 'timeless'. But it does typically reveal a willingness to play – with a detail, an accessory, a way of wearing. Fred Astaire, for example, was at heart a conservative dresser: but using a tie instead of a belt, or a pin to hold the break of his shirt in place, was all it took to make him a man of style.

Indeed, as important as this, men of style are consistent. Not only is their interest in the vagaries of passing fads minimal, but so is changing their way of dress once they have settled on one that works for the way they live. To fashion followers, this is to attire oneself in boredom. For them, the freedom to change the way one dresses is a large part of the pleasure in wearing clothes. And they wouldn't necessarily be wrong. There is much to be said for embracing the wardrobe's rich diversity.

But this is not the man of style's way – which is perhaps why so many of them say (or at least claim) to have little interest in clothes, for all that many reveal clearly how well they know what suits them; Steve McQueen, for instance, wasn't about to let historic accuracy stand in the way of his desire to wear trim, more form-fitting khakis in *The Great Escape*. For them their dress is simply what they wear. For onlookers, it becomes a form of branding, a sartorial signature. That, ultimately, is what lasts (and, of course, it helps if you're devilishly handsome and/or overflowing with charisma, too).

At least it lasts for the figures in this book, but one might well ask for how long. The modern age is, for men, increasingly one that embraces fashion. Revolutions, both industrial and social – from the way the fashion business manufactures and markets its products, to the way men of all ages have been granted permission to care about their appearance and dress in the styles of the season – have in recent years transformed the male wardrobe. The very idea of style is in flux, such that, arguably, it will more and more be conceived of as being associated with fashion, rather than individuality.

Perhaps, in fact, this is why so many of the men cited here as men of style – Fred Astaire, Steve McQueen et al. – have become a kind of canon, the classics that defined cool. This is, in part, a product of rarity – a well-dressed man stands apart, and so is looked to as a touchstone of style for generation after generation. It may also be because they belong to an age when, as far as men had anything more than a practical relationship with their dress, style was all there was. You either had it – and, ideally, the media/public profile to make it known – or you didn't have it. One wasn't in competition with today's world, in which so many more men are concerned about the way they present themselves, and in which many more still are happy to do that wearing the look of the moment.

Perhaps, indeed, this also means that these men of style are enjoying their last hurrah, destined to be outmoded. Not only because – in a digital age in which an appreciation for history is a fragile one, and in which one is bombarded by images of fleetingly fashionable celebrities – fewer and fewer will actually know who they are, but because men's fashion will become more and more pre-eminent.

One hopes they will not be forgotten for their contribution. One hopes, too, that, if the tried-and-tested heroes of men's style in this book are superseded, it is by men who prove inspiring by having an equally long and consistent track record of dressing their own way, rather than the way of everyone else.

GIANNI AGNELLI

1921 – 2003

Gianni Agnelli, in front of a scale model
of the Fiat office tower, in 1972.

Style, undoubtedly, is ably assisted by great wealth. But while Gianni Agnelli, as a member of the founding family of the Fiat industrial empire, would certainly have had money – indeed, at one point he was said to be worth £2 billion, making him the richest man in modern Italian history – that alone could not explain his much-copied idiosyncrasies of dress.

It is often said that you need to know and respect the rules before you break them. And on any other person, the quirks of dress that became Agnelli's signatures might readily be dismissed as silly – or as belonging to someone ill- rather than individually dressed. But perhaps his money, reputation – as much as a playboy as a magnate – and power afforded him a leeway that the less fortunate would not be granted.

Take just a few of Agnelli's sartorial hallmarks as cases in point. He would wear a tie – typically tied using an Italian four-in-hand knot, wrapped twice rather than once around – just a little undone, and a little off-centre, much as a scruffy schoolboy might; said tie might also be worn with the narrow end longer than the blade, considered a faux pas by style etiquette guides. Similarly, as a fan of double-breasted suits, he would occasionally wear these undone, again a look that went against supposed propriety; he would wear the collars of his Brooks

Brothers button-down collared shirts unbuttoned, whether wearing a tie or not.

Other touches were less easy to dismiss simply as errors, and more easy to read as inventiveness. He would wear slipper-like casual shoes, and, more strikingly still, hiking boots with his immaculately tailored bespoke suits. He enthusiastically clashed patterns, especially varieties of check. He loved to leave one or two buttons of his suit jacket's cuffs left undone, a perhaps vulgar – and certainly much imitated – demonstration of his preferred A. Careceni grey flannel tailoring's bespoke quality (this at a time before a working or surgeon's cuff became commonplace on ready-to-wear). Most notably of all, he chose to wear his watch over the top of his buttoned shirt cuff. Agnelli insisted that this was because he didn't even have the time to pull it back when he wanted to see his watch, but the truth – as is often the case with Agnelli – proved to be more prosaic. He is said to have first worn his watch this way after a bespoke dress shirt from Battistoni proved, unlike his Brooks Brothers shirts, to leave insufficient room for it under the cuff. And that penchant for wearing hiking boots with his suits? In 1952 he was involved in a road accident near Monte Carlo that seriously damaged one of his legs – rather than take the option of

Gianni Agnelli, king of industry, standing
in front of the Fiat factory in Turin, 1967.

Gianni Agnelli pictured in 1964, wearing his watch over his shirt cuff.

'THERE ARE
MEN WHO TALK
OF WOMEN AND
OTHERS WHO
TALK TO THEM –
I PREFER TALKING
TO THEM.'

Gianni Agnelli in 1966.

Another touch of personal style: Agnelli teams
hiking boots with a suit.

wearing a brace, he chose instead to wear the kind of boots that gave the right support.

But it still took Agnelli to see that a way of wearing counter to the ordinary or expected could prove a point of distinction. *Life* magazine would in 1967 describe Agnelli as having 'the sculptured bearing of an exquisitely tailored Julius Caesar'. Such distinction certainly suited his reputation as an international man of high taste and high jinks, and during the 1950s to 1970s, the golden era of Europe's most high-glamour partying, he earned the sobriquets, 'the Rake of the Riviera' and 'the Uncrowned King of Italy'.

That car crash, for example, was the result of his driving too fast after a row with his then girlfriend, Pamela Churchill, just one of a string of beauties with whom he was romantically connected over the years (including during his one marriage) – Anita Ekberg, Rita Hayworth and, reputedly, Jackie Kennedy. When Agnelli hosted Kennedy on an official White House visit to Italy, John Kennedy is said to have telegrammed her that she should be enjoying 'more Caroline [the Kennedys' daughter], less Agnelli'.

Agnelli was unrepentant, albeit in a philosophical fashion: 'You could be a good husband and fool around, or a very bad husband and be *fidel*,' he once noted. 'There are men who talk of women and others who talk to them – I prefer talking to them,' he would add. And this from the man who, having been wounded twice on the Russian front during World War II, would receive his third injury being shot by a German officer in a bar over an argument about a woman. Agnelli is said to have managed to finish his drink before leaving. Now that's style.

FRED ASTAIRE

1899 – 1987

Fred Astaire posing for a promotional
shot for the Columbia Pictures film
You'll Never Get Rich, 1941.

Fred Austerlitz, better known as Fred Astaire, was not your obvious fashion plate material. Slender, just 5 feet 9 inches (1.75 metres) tall, with large protruding ears and thinning hair, all factors his early critics seized upon – noting too his high voice – it was perhaps small wonder that Astaire himself never understood being cited as one of the best-dressed men of his era.

'It always comes as a surprise to me,' he said in an interview with *GQ* in 1957. 'I never think of myself as spic and span or all duded out – just as someone who wants to be comfortable and satisfy his own taste.' But therein lay the secret of his sartorial success. Indeed, the style for which, via his many films, the Academy Award-winning actor, singer, dancer and choreographer was best known – the extreme formality of top hat, white tie and tails, made by Savile Row's Anderson & Sheppard – was not one he much appreciated personally. 'Of course,' he said, 'in my business you have to dress for a role. At home, I dress for myself. I don't think I look too well in suits. I'm really quite sloppy – casual, you know. I dress for myself and to feel relaxed.'

He felt this way, perhaps, because he spent so much of his time in what he called 'sweat clothes' – those most comfortable trousers and jackets he wore to rehearse in. But certainly, while many actors have been hailed as style icons for one or a few screen roles – a style they didn't maintain unaided in their personal lives – Astaire was often more stylish off- than on-screen. Although he often bought his shirts off the rack, his dark blue, charcoal and occasionally light grey suiting was typically tailored for him on Savile Row and in Beverly Hills. Subtlety was key: 'I just don't like a suit to stand out. I don't want someone looking twice at me and saying, "What was that?" in an incredulous tone.' But so was exactitude: he said that he typically took his suits back to the tailors at least six times to have adjustments made, noting that he especially disliked wearing 'a lot of material – I don't see any reason to carry all that extra cloth about'.

This was in part to make his suits easier to move in, his grace adding of course to his image of casual elegance. But it was also because, while he dressed in Brooks Brothers in his teenage years, Astaire invariably looked to British traditions of dress for his inspiration. 'You have to give them credit,' he once remarked wryly. 'They have been very stable in their designing and tailoring. They hardly ever change. ... We go away from or towards them in styles, but we always seem to basically revolve around their ideas.'

Astaire certainly developed his own signatures of dress: he would wear a gold pin to hold his shirt together at the desired

Fred Astaire pictured aboard SS *Berengaria*, on arrival in New York City after a European vacation.

Fred Astaire with his dog on the front porch
of his Beverly Hills home, early 1968.

'I DON'T THINK I LOOK
TOO WELL IN SUITS.
I'M REALLY QUITE SLOPPY –
CASUAL, YOU KNOW.'

Fred Astaire in a studio portrait taken in
1950. The pin – used to hold his shirt open
at a certain break – was a signature.

Fred Astaire practises a routine in 1949.
He wears his belt fastened at the side.

A woollen waistcoat gives an informality to Astaire's suit, in this
promotional shot for the Paramount Pictures film *Holiday Inn*, 1942.

break; he wore his trousers cuffed a little shorter than usual; he
might wear brown-suede or white-buckskin Oxford shoes with
no regard for supposed rules of coordinating them with socks
or trousers; he would wear a belt with the buckle pushed to
one side 'simply to get it out of the way' or, more distinctively,
would hold his trousers up by use of a silk scarf or tie – with a
31-inch (79-centimetre) waist and rapidly losing weight during
dance rehearsals, this was, Astaire claimed, the most adaptable
solution.

But beyond these he respected traditions and picked up
ideas from others who inspired him. During the 1920s, Astaire
met the Prince of Wales (later King Edward VIII, then Duke
of Windsor) – then the definitive arbiter of blue-blood good
taste – backstage after a show and consequently would 'get lost

for days in the Burlington Arcade', even suffering the rebuff of
shirt-makers Hawes & Curtis, who declined to make Astaire
a copy of one of the Prince's waistcoats. Although he preferred
a buttoned cuff to a French one, on one occasion Astaire was
inspired to have a pair of diamond and ruby studs made for him
by Cartier. This had been the first thing he had noticed about
the driver of a sports car with whom he had crashed in his
Rolls-Royce in London.

But ultimately Fred Astaire made such inspirations his
own. He wore the clothes. The clothes did not wear him. Indeed,
anecdotally, he was known to throw his new suits against a wall,
as he once joked, 'just to show them who's boss'.

Fred Astaire's style details – tie pin, without a tie, excepting the one he wears as a belt. Shot for the film *Royal Wedding* in 1951.

'DO IT BIG, DO IT RIGHT, AND DO IT WITH STYLE.'

Fred Astaire greets fans on his arrival at Orly Airport in Paris, 1956, where he is due to start filming *Funny Face* with Audrey Hepburn.

Star-spangled socks offset the otherwise muted palette of Astaire's clothing, in *Holiday Inn*, 1942.

FRED ASTAIRE

CHET BAKER

1929 – 1988

Chet Baker, in 1950, wearing a white
T-shirt with his suit – an unusual look
for the times.

Jazz has long been associated with the concept of 'cool' – a cool that comes from the core and that grows out of living apart from the mainstream. Certainly, the great players of jazz from the 1950s to 1960s – chiming with post-war prosperity, the birth of the teenager, the civil rights movement and the spread of TV as mass media – effectively invented the modern idea of cool, with Capitol Records helping to popularize the term with its album *Classics in Jazz: Cool and Quiet*. By association with its performers, and their performances – in smoky, smouldering, ill-lit, gritty, intimate late-night venues, immortalized in evocative monochrome photography – 'cool' came to be associated with the idea of a nonchalant manner and effortless style. Among all of the jazzmen, arguably Chet Baker – self-taught trumpeter and, with Gerry Mulligan, founder of one of the US west coast's most influential quartets – embodied this more than any other.

Jazzmen knew how to dress for the mood. The clothes had to match, in part to sell the complexity of the music. And what better for a sound that was radical than duds that also cut against the grain – by appropriating the Ivy League uniform of the east coast conservative. Yes, the style-seeking jazzmen were building on the shoulders of swing and bebop giants – Louis Armstrong and Duke Ellington were none too sloppy with their

wardrobes either, while Billy Eckstine even designed and wore his own collar shape, the 'Mr B', a high-roll collar that (with some imagination) formed a 'B' shape over a Windsor knot.

What these jazz masters wore, often as signatures, consequently attained an unexpected hipster credibility: Dizzy Gillespie's double-breasted pinstripes, goatee, black horn-rimmed glasses and beret; Stan Getz's dark Italian suits and skinny ties; Lester Young's tilted pork-pie hat; Thelonius Monk, with his outsized specs and beret too. But then there was Henry 'Chet' Baker, playing an easy and light style under the Pacific Jazz label, and reflecting an easy and light mode of dress too.

Look at the cover of *Chet Baker and Crew* and the short-sleeved printed shirts and T-shirts are more surfer dude than New York art house. Add in that Baker had matinee idol looks – that slicked big hair and athletic physique, a jazz James Dean, his only physical flaw said to be a missing incisor, which he lost in a childhood fight and refused to replace lest it affect his playing (ironically his lifelong chronic drug addiction would eventually see all his teeth fall out) – and here was a new, sunnier kind of jazzman in loose gaberdine suits and hand-painted ties. Small wonder then that, when Baker went east, he 'arrived from California dressed like a ragamuffin', as the jazz

Chet Baker, in Lucca, 1961, smartening himself up for his appearance on release after being detained in an Italian prison for drug use.

'PEOPLE SAID I'D NEVER MAKE 35, THEN I'D NEVER MAKE 40, 45; NOW I'M ALMOST 50, SO I'M BEGINNING TO THINK MAYBE THEY MIGHT BE WRONG.'

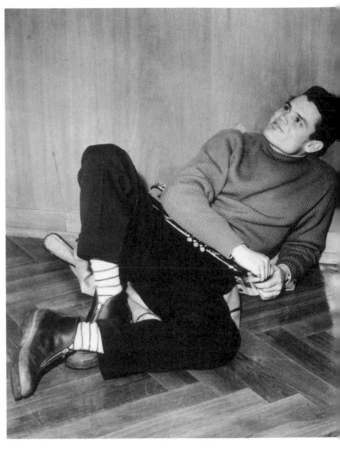

Chet Baker, relaxed in striped socks in 1956.

A still from Bruce Weber's film *Let's Get Lost*, 1988, a more haggard Baker still exuding jazz cool.

promoter Charles Bourgeois put it, with Charlie Davidson, of The Andover Shop, saying of Baker: 'He knew nothing about clothes but he had an innate taste and everything looked great on him. He put on his girlfriend's sweater once and the damned thing looked great on him.'

But arguably attempts to get Baker to stick to the style in which Bourgeois had him kitted out – in repp tie, button-down shirt, navy blazer and Oxfords – did not stick. Baker gravitated back to a more relaxed mode of dress: at its dressiest, the minimalistic dark suit, white T-shirt, thick white socks and black slides that became something of a signature, but more typically in khakis, jeans, tennis shoes and soft sweaters as he might have worn back out west, as he does on the cover of *Chet*. It was a clean-cut look that was suitably uncomplicated – Baker professed to have not only little knowledge of but also little interest in clothes – and somewhat at odds with the reality of his drug-addled, messy life behind the scenes. Ultimately, Baker didn't look to clothes as a means to reflect his sense of self. He had his trumpet for that. 'I don't believe that jazz will ever really die,' he noted. 'It's a nice way to express yourself.'

Chet Baker backstage in his dressing room after performing in London in 1979 – note how the pattern in his V-neck sweater echoes the herringbone of his jacket.

CHET BAKER

CECIL BEATON

1904 – 1980

Cecil Beaton, with Baba Beaton (left)
and Nancy Beaton (right), at the Eton vs
Harrow cricket match at Lord's, London,
during the 1920s.

A practised sense of style might well be an essential trait of anyone whose friend would describe them as being a 'total self-creation', as the writer Truman Capote did of photographer Cecil Beaton. Vanity may be another trait – and Beaton was reportedly well versed in that: a slim man, he had his clothes made a size too small to exaggerate the fact.

Indeed, perhaps it was his own self-absorption – and insecurity about his place in a high-society world of which he was not quite a part – that made him notoriously catty about everyone else and their appearance despite also having a reputation for producing extremely flattering portraits. 'Malice in Wonderland' as he was described by Jean Cocteau, whose surrealistic art techniques were lifted by Beaton to make his photographs more interesting still. The flattery, by many accounts, was more Machiavellian than heartfelt. The publisher George Weidenfeld noted that Beaton would 'happily have witnessed their execution as long as he was given a good enough seat'.

As for his own style, Beaton was always ready to give a twist to a style of dress essentially rooted in tailoring – he was an on-off client of Savile Row's Huntsman, Henry Poole and

Anderson & Sheppard – growing more adventurous and more Edwardian in flavour as the years passed. Indeed, in 1965, he criticized London's tailors for their traditionalism: 'It is ridiculous that they go on turning out clothes that make men look like characters from P. G. Wodehouse. I'm terribly bored with their styling – so behind the times. They really should pay attention to the mods – the barriers are down and everything goes.' That said, when he tried a more continental, modish style – a suit by Pierre Cardin – he castigated himself for being 'foolish enough' to pay twice as much as he normally paid his tailors.

Beaton had been more avant-garde himself before, of course: as one of the 'Bright Young Things' in his youth, he was comfortable in costume and make-up – he threw celebrated *fêtes champêtres* over an evening during which he might change four times into ever more outlandish outfits. One, the so-called 'rabbit coat', was made of corduroy with muslin roses, and was decorated with plastic eggshells. Such a provocative style, however, he toned down in order to fit better into the society he wished to photograph. By the time he was named

A self-portrait by Cecil Beaton,
shot during the 1930s.

Cecil Beaton supervises the fitting of a costume he designed for actress Danielle Volle, for a production of *The School for Scandal*, ca.1960.

'BE ANYTHING THAT WILL ASSERT INTEGRITY OF PURPOSE AND IMAGINATIVE VISION AGAINST THE PLAY-IT-SAFERS, THE CREATURES OF THE COMMONPLACE, THE SLAVES OF THE ORDINARY.'

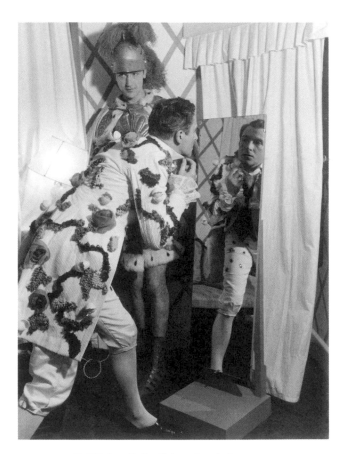

Cecil Beaton adjusting his fancy dress for the summer party at his country house in Ashcombe, 1937.

Cecil Beaton and Mrs Harrison Williams take a walk, Palm Beach, Florida, in 1936. Mrs Williams was named best-dressed woman in the world in 1933 – a more casual Beaton gives her some competition.

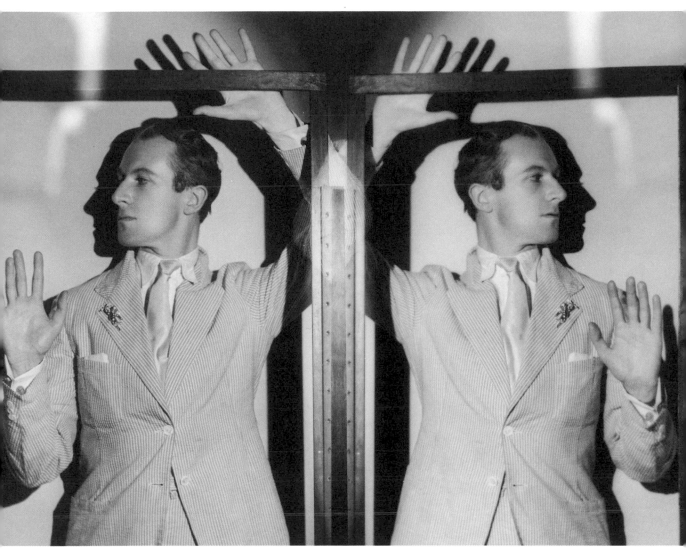

Beaton strikes a dramatic pose in 1930 – note the cufflinks and the brooch on his lapel.

on the International Best-Dressed List of 1970 – alongside the likes of Gianni Agnelli – he was returning to a more subtle flamboyance: large neck scarves in yellows and pinks; patterned socks, with loafers (not a common choice at the time); a selection of more colourful clothes, often in contrasting textures; and broad-brimmed hats all became trademark staples.

Like many outsiders, Beaton professed a determination to be different: 'Be anything that will assert integrity of purpose and imaginative vision against the play-it-safers, the creatures of the commonplace, the slaves of the ordinary,' he said. He lived in the high style of many of his subjects – in suites at top hotels, where he decorated the rooms to demonstrate his interior design flair, with a rococo style to which he later gave full vent at his London and country homes.

But Beaton's interest in fashion was more than personal: he developed a real expertize in the aesthetics of clothing, designed costumes – most notably for *Gigi* and for *My Fair Lady*, for which he won Oscars – and persuaded London's Victoria and Albert Museum to host the first fashion exhibition in a major museum, reflective of his belief that fashion was an art form. As for his definition of elegance, that was simple: 'soap and water'.

CECIL BEATON

GEORGE BEST

1946 – 2005

George Best at his clothes shop George
Best Boutique in Sale, Manchester, 1966.
A flock of willing girls would typically be
waiting outside to catch a glimpse.

Some have argued that, while George Best was undoubtedly one of the greatest players football has known, his status outside the sport was a matter of good timing: a man who embraced his hedonistic excesses, his famous line, 'I spent a lot of money on booze, birds and fast cars. The rest I just squandered,' captured the freewheeling spirit of the late 1960s that were his heyday. At any later time, that freedom to break the mould of conservatism that had long shaped life in the UK – and even more so in his native Northern Ireland – might have been castigated rather than celebrated. Instead there are tales of waiters delivering champagne to Best's hotel room to find the player, in every sense, on the bed with Miss World and thousands of pounds in casino winnings. 'Mr Best, where did it all go wrong?' came the waiter's witty question.

Indeed, here was a footballer who parlayed his skill on the field into a greater cultural status. This was as a figurehead not only for fast living – 'In 1969 I gave up women and alcohol – it was the worst 20 minutes of my life,' he once quipped – nor only for the new celebrity society (besieged by women, he lived under police protection and hired three full-time staffers to answer the 10,000 letters he received every week) but also for style. And this not just on the pitch, though he is said to have started a trend for wearing his shirt outside his shorts, not

tucked in as propriety dictated. What the handsome Best wore off the pitch – whether it was a simple Henley shirt, pink tie-dye, V-neck T-shirt, denim jacket with formal shirt and trousers or a double-breasted velour jacket, or wearing his hair longer than most men in football – invariably informed the wardrobes of men in their twenties at the time.

Indeed, it was the first time a sports star would have such a profound impact on fashion or, perhaps, that fashion would have such an impact on a sports star: commenting that 'if I'd been born ugly, you'd never have heard of Pelé', Best once conceded that his interest in the high life had a detrimental effect on his career. 'Footballers are more interested in fashion than before,' Best commented in 2004. 'Not all of them are David Beckham. Some have no idea. But they get photographed all the time and you see them out, shopping with their wives. It wasn't like that in my day.' Fashion entrepreneur Harold Tillman recruited Best for football's first ever fashion-related endorsement deal – in fact, Best's name would be licensed to fashion manufacturers long after his death in 2005, aged just 59.

Certainly the fifth Beatle, as the Portuguese press dubbed Best, dressed as much like a rock star as a football player: on returning to London from Lisbon he stepped on to the airport's tarmac wearing a leather trench coat and a sombrero. From

George Best at Manchester United FC, in 1966.

George Best and Mike Summerbee, the Manchester City player, may have been sporting rivals, but they joined forces in business to open Edwardia, specializing in Edwardian clothes. Pictured here in 1967.

George Best – sometimes dubbed the fifth Beatle – makes adjustments to his 'Beatle'-style haircut in a mirror, 1964.

George Best, a blend of period tailoring and 1970s hair and beard. His companions are unimpressed …

1967, in partnership with fellow player Mike Summerbee, Best even opened a chain of his own menswear boutiques, called Edwardia, Rogue and George Best Boutique – the first being on Bridge Street in Manchester, the city for which he gave the best part of his playing career. Hair salons and nightclubs followed, opened by Best with his personal hairdresser Malcolm Wagner. 'We thought that we had invented glamour,' as Summerbee would later note of their partnership in an article for *The Independent*. The menswear stores were not successful, in business terms, but then Best once admitted that their main purpose was to attract female attention.

Best continued to enjoy his position as a cheeky, rebel outsider throughout his life. In 2000, he caused a stir by criticizing fellow footballer and trendsetter David Beckham, albeit for his playing skills. 'He cannot kick with his left foot,' Best noted. 'He cannot head a ball. He cannot tackle and he doesn't score many goals. Apart from that, he's all right.'

'IN 1969 I GAVE UP WOMEN AND ALCOHOL – IT WAS THE WORST 20 MINUTES OF MY LIFE.'

George Best, smartly tailored at the Old Trafford ground, on his way to an away match during the 1970s. He carries his kit in his Puma bag.

GEORGE BEST

DAVID BOWIE

1947 — 2016

A vibrant and streamlined David Bowie
with dyed red hair, braces and
a mustard-yellow suit, in 1974.

David Bowie worked as hard in creating his wardrobe as he did his music. Indeed, if other men embodied a certain style and made it their own, Bowie proved a chameleon, shifting his look as frequently, and as easily, as a shift in tempo, using clothing more as a form of role play. Ziggy Stardust, Aladdin Sane, the monochromatic Thin White Duke – these personae reeled from sharp-dressed gent to circus performer, dapper to freakish, on each occasion forming a key element of his stagecraft, projecting identity and playing with the idea of what it was to be a rock star. 'I'm a person who can take on the guises of different people that I meet. ... I take on their accent. ... I'm a collector,' as the performer once said of himself.

That ability evolved with his music – the early David Bowie of the mid 1960s wore everyday slim suit and tie, as befitted the mod-inflected times, even if his hair was, also for the times, on the long side. 'I think we're all fairly tolerant,' he said during his first TV appearance, aged 17, in which he billed himself as the spokesman for the 'Society for the Prevention of Cruelty to Long-Haired Men'. 'But for the last two years we've had comments like "Darlin" and "Can I carry your handbag?" thrown at us, and I think it just has to stop now.' Rather, he stopped caring.

By 1971 – following his introduction to dancer and mime artist Lindsay Kemp, with whom Bowie was keen to explore how these art forms might be blended with rock and roll, and with the release of *Hunky Dory* – a transformed Bowie began to bend the gender stereotypes in long hair, flared trousers and blousy shirt, to try on different looks. His first wife, Angie Barnett, would assist in and encourage her husband's play with androgyny – the 'man dresses' as Bowie would call the styles made for him by London tailor Michael Fish and worn on the cover of *The Man Who Sold the World*. 'As long as he remains a boy, I can't see any harm in it,' his own mother noted.

Thus was set a pattern of regular, almost annual image overhauls – for each album, a new fashion concept. A year later and the man-woman was more alien, with the arrival of Ziggy Stardust's glam excesses – a hotchpotch of all of Bowie's influences and interests, make-up inspired by Alice Cooper, outfits via Stanley Kubrick's *A Clockwork Orange*, hair colour by model Marie Helvin, hair cut courtesy of Evelyn Paget ladies' hair salon on Beckenham High Street – much of the Ziggy stage persona designed by Kansai Yamamoto, who Bowie had spotted at the first Japanese fashion show in the UK.

The turns of style came suddenly. Come 1974 and Bowie was in piratical eyepatch, knotted top and hip-hugging, cropped dungarees. Come 1976 and any hint of Ziggy or Aladdin were

David Bowie in Amsterdam, 1974,
complete with his iconic eyepatch.

'I DON'T KNOW WHERE I'M GOING FROM HERE, BUT I PROMISE IT WON'T BE BORING.'

David Bowie blends big pattern and big boots, while being interviewed at home in Beckenham, London, in April 1972.

dead. A more soulful Bowie appeared with slicked-back hair, elegant in open-neck shirt and blazer, the beginnings of a less obviously theatrical, more comparatively conservative style that still played brilliantly with silhouette, proportion and meaning. The showbiz of knitted leotard and asymmetric catsuit, sequins and platform boots had given way to a style informed by German Expressionism, *Cabaret*, perhaps the jazz greats of the 1940s and 1950s – their boxy suits, braces, loosened ties, trench coats, fedoras – and cocaine use. During his Thin White Duke phase Bowie had a 26-inch (66-centimetre) waist.

Not that a new maturity meant Bowie had put away all temptations towards more outlandish dress. Pierrot-inspired costumes and even a so-called 'cyber-clown' style were among those to make showings over subsequent decades. These may have proven less influential on fashion at large than previous outfits, but there was little doubting that fashion would always be watching.

David Bowie in a tan suit and a white belt, 1983. Note how Bowie tucks the jacket into his trousers to create a boiler suit effect.

Slicked back, formal yet romantic, David Bowie prefigures New Romanticism as the Thin White Duke, on stage in Copenhagen, 1976.

Bowie – on the right – with wife Angie and three-week-old son Zowie, in 1971. Bowie bends genders in Oxford bag trousers, Turkish cotton shirt and a felt hat.

DAVID BOWIE

MICHAEL CAINE

b. 1933

Michael Caine as Harry Palmer in one
of the films that defined his look,
The Ipcress File, in 1965.

David Bailey's portrait of Michael Caine, taken in 1965, would become an image that defined both the actor and the decade. But it also helped form Caine's place as a symbol of the sartorial and societal shifts of the time – away from the Establishment and privilege and towards youth and talent. Caine was not only a cockney who sounded like one but, cutting against received wisdom as to just what a film star should look like, as Buddy Holly had done for a rock 'n' roll star, he also wore heavy black spectacles.

He even had to overcome his blonde hair: 'There were no heroes with blonde hair,' Caine once noted in an interview with *New York* magazine. 'Robert Taylor and Henry Fonda, they all had dark hair. The only one I found was Van Johnson, who wasn't too cool. He was a nice, homely American boy. So I created my own image. It worked.'

Indeed, Caine's style was more than his specs: through his place at the heart of the Swinging Sixties – sharing a flat with Terence Stamp in an era in which, Caine once noted, everyone you knew was set to become famous – the actor's dress represented a new era. It was a smart, suited, continental, photographic look – a product perhaps of Caine's understanding of the big screen, as one of the first British actors to go global without coming up through the theatre.

Caine had a long personal and working relationship with the influential Mayfair tailor Douglas Hayward, who advocated, as Caine noted, a 'very close-fitting', more body-conscious tailoring of short, double-vented jackets and narrow trousers. Typically, he avoided suede shoes at all costs. John Wayne had once advised Caine not to wear them, 'because one day, Michael, you'll be taking a piss, and the guy next to you will recognize you, and he'll turn toward you and say "Michael Caine!" and piss all over your shoes'.

'He was much more than a tailor [his premises were] a gathering place,' Caine recalled of Hayward. 'Whenever you were away you came in here and saw everybody, just sitting around [on the] sofas. ... It was like a club. His clientele were not people out to do press with their clothing, they were out to dress well and feel good, which we did, and do.'

It helped, of course, that so many of Caine's roles of the era – in films such as *The Ipcress File*, *Funeral in Berlin*, *Alfie* (the central character is said to have been inspired by Hayward), *The Italian Job* and *Get Carter* – were so stylish in their costume. As Charlie Croker, mastermind of the Italian job, said on release from prison, 'Take me to my tailor!': Adrian, said tailor, is quick to dismiss Croker's old two-piece as 'quite revolting' and, via Hayward of course, creates a veritable catwalk of

Classic fitted double-breasted tailoring of the mid 1960s, worn with a loosened tie by Caine during a photo shoot at the Plaza Hotel in New York.

Arguably Caine's most seminal on-screen
suit, for *The Italian Job*, in 1969.

'I'M EVERY BOURGEOIS NIGHTMARE – A COCKNEY WITH INTELLIGENCE AND A MILLION DOLLARS.'

influential suits, culminating in one of the most celebrated in cinema history, namely a three-button beige linen style that epitomized the era.

Then, as Harry Palmer in the films of Len Deighton's spy stories, Caine plays the slightly shabby antidote to James Bond, in tweed jacket, thin knitted tie, mac and spectacles. In *Get Carter* Caine wears a dark blue three-piece suit and black silk tie that, like much of the actor's own attire, avoided current trends – the wide lapels, high shirt collars and flared trousers of the 1970s, in this case – in favour of the updated classic. As Caine said of Hayward's work, capturing his own style dictum, 'It was brilliant tailoring that didn't draw any attention to itself whatsoever.'

Michael Caine as the anti-Bond Harry Palmer
– shabby and ordinary in glasses and mac, in a
scene from the film *Funeral in Berlin* in 1966.

Michael Caine, photographed for the *Sunday Times* in 1965,
his trademark heavy frames in place.

MICHAEL CAINE

TRUMAN CAPOTE

1924 – 1984

Buttoned up, a young Truman Capote in
Venice, Italy, in 1955.

'Style,' the writer Truman Capote once said, 'is what you are.'
That is a bold statement, but it was a reflection of Capote's
psyche, and especially of his fascination (one arguably stemming
from his own sense of inadequacies deriving from his upper-
middle-class roots) with the very rich. 'There's no taste in
middle-class rich,' he noted. 'You must be either very rich or
very poor. There's absolutely no taste in between. The freedom
to pursue an aesthetic quality in life is an extra dimension. Why
not create a whole aesthetic ambience? Be your own living work
of art?' Capote, the public figure, certainly, was the result of an
act of self-creation. 'I am not a saint yet,' he wrote in *Music for
Chameleons*. 'I'm an alcoholic. I'm a drug addict. I'm homosexual.
I'm a genius.'

Capote was a small man – just 5 feet 3 inches (1.6 metres):
'about as tall as a shotgun and just as noisy,' as he put it – but
he made up for it with a big, outrageously gossipy character
which won him as many enemies as friends (when Capote died,
fellow writer Gore Vidal called it 'a good career move'). Lots

of hats also helped – self-conscious about his height, he wore
every kind of hat, from fedoras to baseball caps, boaters to, more
rakishly, sailor's caps.

Indeed, the author of *Breakfast at Tiffany's* and *In Cold
Blood* regarded clothes as a carapace both behind which he could
deflect attention from his flaws, including a high-pitched voice
and strange inflection to his speech, and one through which he
could project a version of himself more suitable to the high-
society company he kept – and fed, notably through his Black
and White Ball, an event that became so prestigious one heiress
threatened to kill herself unless she got an invitation.

When he wasn't in Alfred Dunhill dinner dress, Capote
favoured white suits and bow ties – a nod, perhaps, to America's
literary heavyweight Mark Twain – but was at home in pastel
linens or a Breton top. Pre-war, Ivy League preppy style mixed
with aristocratic flair saw Fair Isle sweaters and club collar shirts
as much part of his wardrobe as tweed jackets and Prince Albert
slippers. His was a style, and a physique, distinctive enough that

Capote, photographed in 1948.

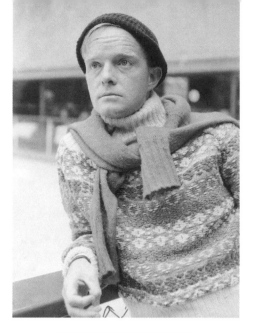

Truman Capote in layered woollens at the
Rockefeller ice skating rink, New York.

Truman Capote in a hat – it made him feel taller – even
while at home, in Sagaponack, Long Island, 1971, and in
front of his bookcase, below left, 23 years earlier.

'I'M AN ALCOHOLIC. I'M A DRUG ADDICT. I'M HOMOSEXUAL. I'M A GENIUS.'

Round glasses, striped T-shirt, jeans with turn-ups
– Capote affects a literary beatnik style, 1950.

it could make for a good joke: in Woody Allen's *Annie Hall*, there is a scene in which the two main characters are watching strangers go by. 'Oh,' says one, 'there's the winner of the Truman Capote lookalike contest.' The passer-by is Capote, who appeared uncredited.

In one of his letters, later collected and published in *Too Brief a Treat*, Capote wrote enthusiastically, and in detail, about his plans for new clothes. 'I've started myself a new wardrobe – a foolhardy enterprise considering my finances. First off, I sent my measurements to Ferragamo in Florence and he has made me the most beautiful pair of black shoes ... Then I've had three suits made out of a strange kind of flat velvet – to die.' In another letter he writes that it has occurred to him that he will also require something for 'promenading in the piazza': 'I should adore to wear the orange-lined cloak,' he writes. 'I do feel the need of something spectacular.'

TRUMAN CAPOTE

JOHNNY CASH

1932 – 2003

Johnny Cash – cowboy balladeer – at a
ranch in San Antonio, Texas, in 1959.

Long before Japanese designers revived black as the definitive fashion colour during the 1980s, one man made it his own. 'Hello, I'm Johnny Cash,' as the rockabilly/country music star would typically introduce his performances – typically too dressed head to toe in the darkest shade. But behind this unusual choice – the 1940s and 1950s saw a spurt of vibrant hues, from the big screen to the candy-coloured goods of America's post-war consumer boom – was a deeper meaning.

It was, Cash once said, a good luck charm, following his wearing a black T-shirt and jeans for his first public performance. More frequently he said it was to stand as a symbol of support for all of the oppressed. 'I wore black because I liked it,' Cash explained. 'Wearing it still means something to me. It's still my symbol of rebellion – against a stagnant status quo, against our hypocritical houses of God, against people whose minds are closed to others' ideas.'

In the lyrics to 'Man in Black' – which by then had long become a nickname for him – Cash described the reason for his 'sombre tone': he wears black 'for the poor and the beaten down', for those who are 'held back'. Indeed, he sings how nobody will

see him in white until such social ills are resolved. That choice, however, also made his style – limited as it subsequently was – a new benchmark, both in fashion and on the stage. If other performers opted for glitzy, more glamorous attire – think of Little Richard's signature purple jacket, or Elvis' gold lamé suit – Cash stood in stark contrast.

The decision to adopt black was, though, not his – and the justification Cash gave for it in song form was retrofitted. Sometimes referred to as 'The Rhinestone Rembrandt', Nashville-based Mexican costumier Manuel – he went by the single name and specialized in western attire – was responsible for outfitting the likes of Hank Williams and Bob Dylan, for The Rolling Stones and the Grateful Dead. He made that golden suit for Elvis, and Richard's jacket. 'Record companies call me to help fabricate personalities for their artists,' as Manuel has explained. 'I do for artists what they need – not what they think they need.' And so he did for Johnny Cash.

'Johnny Cash was so surprised,' Manuel once recalled. 'He said, "Brother, how come you made me nine outfits but they're all black?" I started kidding with him. I said, "There was

Johnny Cash in his trademark black,
brooding in the recording studio, 1960s.

Johnny Cash performs at the A. P. Carter Memorial Festival in Maces Springs, Virginia, 1977. A. P. Carter was the leader of the American country music pioneers the Carter Family – Cash was married to June Carter.

'SOMETIMES I AM TWO PEOPLE. JOHNNY IS THE NICE ONE. CASH CAUSES ALL THE TROUBLE. THEY FIGHT.'

Western style meets tuxedoed rock 'n' roll – Cash with Elvis Presley in 1955. Note the detail of Cash's hand-embroidered shirt.

a special on black fabric ..." I told him, "I think that you're the man in black. You should wear this colour. It's your vibe, it's your aura. Something tells me you should wear this colour." He said, "All right, I'll try it."' And Cash liked it – black trousers and cowboy boots, with the show-business element found in a more fancifully decorated black tailored jacket or western shirt.

Cash returned to Manuel instructing him to make outfits weekly, and this time 'the colour is not in question any more'. Add black sunglasses, often Ray-Ban Wayfarers, and the brooding style was set. 'I'm so uncomfortable wearing colours in public, even denim,' Cash would comment decades later, in 1996. 'Almost everything I've got [has got] black on.'

The Man in Black on his day off, on the streets in 1968.

JOHNNY CASH

WINSTON CHURCHILL

1874 – 1965

A young Churchill shortly after he deserted the Conservative and Unionist Party to become a Liberal, in 1904.

The Winston Churchill leading Britain through World War II cut a striking figure, stylistically speaking: the heavy three-piece suits – which, when he once posed with a Thompson sub-machine gun, lent an air of Hollywood gangster about him, as Nazi propaganda noted; the gold watch chain – to which was attached a family heirloom, the Breguet pocket watch, as well as various keepsakes, including a silver head of Napoleon and a medallion from a by-election he had lost in 1924; the dotted bow ties, like his father's; the John Bull hat (a short top hat more typical of the Edwardian age) or the grey homburg; and the trademark cigars, preferably Cuban brands Camacho or Romeo y Julieta, though, when times were hard, buying (literally by the thousand) cheap American cigars in secret from the Equitable Cigar Stand on Broadway, New York.

But Churchill understood that many such items, cigars especially, were as much a theatrical prop as something simply to smoke, his bodyguard speculating that, while one was always at hand, perhaps five a day were destroyed by chewing, frequent relighting and dropping. Similarly, while Churchill loved uniforms – he had, at various times, at least one for each of the services – his favourite was said to be one of his own design: a distinctive zip-up all-in-one, not unlike a child's 'romper', which he dubbed the 'siren suit' and which would become something

of a totem for a nation to rally around in wartime.

It was inspired by the boiler suits worn by bricklayers working at his country home before World War II – Churchill, as well as being a statesman, bibliophile, painter and writer, was also a keen bricklayer – and proved a useful means of getting dressed quickly when air-raid sirens sounded, thrown on with his monogrammed slippers or zip-up boots. Naturally, Churchill's siren suits were made for him by Jermyn Street shirt-makers Turnbull & Asser in a generous cut with plenty of pockets, and in a variety of fabrics – in a smock material to paint in, in a blue serge or in pinstripes for more businesslike meetings, even in red, green or blue velvet for dressier occasions.

The symbolic power of well-chosen attire or accessory was not new to Churchill either. Indeed, as a young man at the front during World War I, he wore uniform bought privately from Fortnum & Mason, but greatly enjoyed the gift of a 'fine steel helmet' from the French: 'I look most martial in it – like a Cromwellian,' he wrote. 'I always intend to wear it under fire – but chiefly for the appearance.'

Dressing up was something his class was skilled at and his position required. As a parliamentarian he had long taken on the full attire of the gentleman – suits and (often fur-collared astrakhan) overcoats from London tailors Bernau &

Churchill gives the famous victory sign as he
leaves Number 10 Downing Street, in late 1944.

Winston Churchill in his trademark homburg
and bow-tie, at Westminster in 1937.

Churchill relaxes in his siren suit, a one-piece garment of his own design, to be put on in a hurry if required in the middle of the night.

'MY TASTES ARE SIMPLE: I AM EASILY SATISFIED WITH THE BEST.'

Churchill with a Thompson sub-machine gun, during the 1940s – the German propagandists used the image to portray Churchill as a 'gangster'.

Sons or Henry Poole, canes and umbrellas by Thomas Brigg & Sons, hats by Chapman & Moore, boots by Palmer & Co., his preferred grey antelope slippers by Hook, Knowles & Co. Such was the litany of respected makers making for the well-to-do man about London town – right down to his underwear. Churchill's wife, Clementine, bemoaned that he was 'most extravagant about his underclothes': he preferred underwear and nightshirts (never pyjamas) in pale pink silk, which he insisted was important given his delicate skin.

Such choices mattered – as a public figure they certainly came under scrutiny. 'One of the greatest failures as a wedding garment we have ever seen, giving the wearer a sort of glorified coachman appearance,' sniffed *Tailor & Cutter* magazine of Churchill's wedding suit. But, perhaps more importantly, while Churchill was no fop – to him clothing was, above all, utilitarian – clothing mattered to him. He rarely travelled light, for instance. And, as noted in Barry Singer's *Churchill Style*, even as a 15-year-old student at Harrow, he wrote home to his mother offering rather laborious details of his attire: 'I have ordered 1 pair of trousers, 1 pair of knickerbockers, 1 jacket & 1 Waistcoat all of the same stuff. I enclose a pattern. They have not yet begun to make it so you can change it if you wish. They fully understand the making of Knee Breeches. Nice & Bagsy over knee.'

GARY COOPER

1901 – 1961

Gary Cooper posing for a
studio portrait in 1934.

Few men have been immortalized for their style in an Irving Berlin standard, as Cooper was in 'Puttin' On the Ritz', let alone one that would be sung by the ever-stylish Fred Astaire. But in the 1930s, when the classic tune was a hit, Gary Cooper was the height of fashion and had already proved himself both a silent-screen star and one never inelegantly dressed at that.

Indeed, his style set him aside from his contemporaries perhaps – as his daughter, Maria Cooper Janis, would later theorize – because his three years of private schooling in England (from where his father had emigrated) had given him a more nonchalant, European flair. It was certainly a long way, sartorially, from his native Montana. Those three years had also seen Cooper involved in a near-fatal car accident, following which his doctor ordered horseback riding several times a week as a form of therapy; years later, Cooper, some short-lived jobs behind him, including that as a theatrical curtains salesman, got work as a horse-riding extra in cowboy films. Even the limp would be reworked more as a lopsided strut.

Come 1939, Cooper was the world's highest-paid actor with his best work – in the films *The Westerner*, *Sergeant York*, *For Whom the Bell Tolls*, *The Fountainhead* and *High Noon* – all yet to come. In later life, famous friends would include such diverse and artistic types as Frank Sinatra, Pablo Picasso and Ernest Hemingway, who only added to his allure. Having taken a sabbatical from acting to tour Continental Europe for a year, he had developed a taste for Rome's best tailors, who only added to his style.

'I never saw him not look put together. He would never have gone on a television talk show without having a jacket and tie,' as Janis said of her father. 'Even when he was young he would know what was proper for the occasion and he would act accordingly.' And Cooper, note, belonged to an era in which film stars – the men most significantly – typically chose their own attire. This should have proven a disaster – after all, Cooper once told a magazine that he did 'not know a darn thing about dressing'. But this was clearly masculinity speaking.

'He wore the clothes; the clothes did not wear him,' Janis also stressed of the man who was as at ease in woodsman garb as he was top hat and tails or, indeed, his style signatures: broad-shouldered, waisted, wide-lapelled suits; ample trousers with

Gary Cooper wearing a denim shirt – but teamed
with a dashing silk ascot – in 1940.

Gary Cooper ponders a script, 1931 – note the coordinated tie and braces.

Studio portraits from the late 1930s, above and right. Note the styling details – sweater tucked into trousers in one, and tie worn as belt (as Fred Astaire did) in the other.

Cooper aboard USS *Europa* as it came into New York in 1932. Cooper was returning from a big game hunt – he was said to have returned with a staggering 50 lion and other animal skins.

turn-ups; horizontally striped socks; gently clashing patterns. 'He didn't have a dresser. You had to have your own taste and your own style and you chose what you wanted. He knew what he liked in fabric and colour, texture and style. And he sought out different designers and had them make what he wanted. At six foot four [1.93 metres] and very slim, he wasn't hard to dress.'

Cooper was even known to make clothes himself, notably those for comfortable wear on the 600-acre (243-hectare) family ranch – fringed buckskin jackets and Indian moccasins, which he would soak in warm water and allow to shrink-to-fit around his feet. He also preferred his denim looking worn – he would beat new jeans against a rock and leave them in the sun to age them a little. 'Coop', as he was known to his friends, was more down-to-earth than Hollywood usually allowed.

GARY COOPER

GABRIELE D'ANNUNZIO

1863 – 1938

Gabriele D'Annunzio, in trademark
exaggerated collar and lapels.

Prolific poet, prince, politician; rampant philanderer, *flâneur* and fame-hunter; home decorator, thrill-seeker, romantic, rogue; con man, cocaine addict, social climber and proto-Fascist – Gabriele D'Annunzio was a self-made man in a quite literal way, unflaggingly conscious of his image to the point of preposterous vanity. He declared himself Italy's greatest poet since Dante, and likened himself to Caesar, Nelson and Byron. He wrote to the newspapers giving news of his own tragic death in a fall from a horse in advance of the release of his first publication, just to drum up publicity.

Much as his often violent and sexually explicit books titillated, so D'Annunzio himself aimed to make a quick and forceful impression: short, balding, with discoloured teeth and a high-pitched voice, he countered his inadequacies by always being dressed formally and immaculately, with small, if noticeable, excesses that fed his desire for self-promotion. His club collars, of which he was particularly fond, were just that little bit larger than normal, his bow tie just that extra touch more flamboyant, the favoured peaked lapels of his jacket always slightly wider than typical. His use of the latest pomades and

colognes – he liked the scent of oranges – was noted, and he refused to wear any item of clothing that was not imported.

D'Annunzio's flair for a life lived in the grand posture did not only stop at his clothing but included his surroundings too. He would buy thousands of books. On one shopping trip he bought twenty-two dogs and eight horses. When he stayed in hotels, he always travelled with his own sheets. 'I am,' he once explained with characteristic self-assuredness, 'a better decorator and upholsterer than I am a poet or novelist.'

Indeed, at the turn of the century, when his marriage into aristocracy, and his journalism and plays afforded him considerable wealth, he typically lived in rented furnished houses, which, at great expense, he immediately refurbished in extravagant fashion. Or, as he put it, in a style 'gorgeous enough to be worthy of a Renaissance lord'. This involved both filling them with mock-sixteenth-century furniture of his own design, and keeping the interior at near-tropical temperatures. Perhaps this explains his enthusiasm for wearing little more than a kimono-style gown around the house.

Indeed, D'Annunzio's sense both for the luxurious and for

Even fresh from a swim and wrapped in a sheet,
D'Annunzio pulled off a certain style.

'Poet and Italian Patriot' was the title
of this portrait of D'Annunzio.

'AM I NOT THE PRECURSOR OF ALL THAT IS GOOD ABOUT FASCISM?'

D'Annunzio's dandy-lover credentials
lent themselves to parody – a cartoonist
shows him powdering his face in a hand
mirror with wings growing from his back
and Cupid's arrows lying on the floor.

D'Annunzio in a wide-brimmed hat with two of his
many dogs, in the gardens of the Vittoriale.

A dandy at home – D'Annunzio at La Capponcina, during the 1890s.

role play never really left him. Towards the end of his life he took to wearing a simple Franciscan monk's habit – an outward suggestion of penitence perhaps. Underneath said habit, however, D'Annunzio was always sure to wear a pricey mauve silk shirt.

His deeply ingrained love of the idea of romantic recklessness did, however, find real manifestation, even a kind of greatness. He worked with Debussy on a musical setting for one of his poems, but casually turned down Puccini's request that he write the libretto for an opera. He became an avid aviator – seeing the pioneering pilots as modern knights.

On hearing that the Treaty of Versailles would cede the Dalmatian port of Fiume to the new Yugoslavia, he cobbled together a 2,000-strong private army of loyal followers – as star-struck by his magnetic personality as, despite his unprepossessing looks, many women were – and marched on, seized, annexed and proclaimed the city an independent state. He declared himself to be its *Duce* and ran the show with the help of an elite corps of soldiers that he dubbed, with the usual theatricality, the 'Centurions of Death'.

This situation held for two years until the nitty-gritty of achieving ends through political expediency – never D'Annunzio's strong suit – became too much and he left for Venice, not so much even pursued let alone prosecuted. But even this adventure became an opportunity to make a sartorial statement. All of his followers dressed to his design: a black and silver uniform, topped with a black fez. His on-off friend, and perhaps protégé, one Benito Mussolini, looked on; soon after he and his blackshirts seized power in Rome and took on not just D'Annunzio's dark style (*sans* fez), but the straight-armed salute and the glorification of both virility and country.

'Am I not the precursor of all that is good about Fascism?' D'Annunzio wrote to Il Duce in 1932, a hint perhaps that, had he acted, it could have been him at the capital – a turn of events that, since he couldn't stand Hitler, could have shaped global history.

GABRIELE D'ANNUNZIO

MILES DAVIS

1926 – 1991

A candid 1950s portrait of Miles Davis,
in preppy knitwear.

Miles Davis thanked his mother. 'She had a whole lot of style,' the pioneering jazz trumpeter recalled in *Miles: The Autobiography*. 'She had mink coats, diamonds. She was a very glamorous woman who was into all kinds of hats and things, and my mother's friends seemed just as glamorous to me as she was. She was always dressed to kill. I got my looks from my mother and also my love of clothes and sense of style.'

And what a sense of style that was. Look to the 1970s and Davis is an archetype of the superfly – Afro hair, big fur coats, kick flares, stacked-heel shoes, flamboyant scarves, outsized sunglasses. Once discovered, in fact, Davis was rarely seen without statement sunglasses, one official line being that it helped combat shyness when performing, the unofficial line being that it prevented his direct, intense, often cold stare from starting fights. Borrowing from any source – from the Paris catwalks to Haight-Ashbury's street scene – Davis would dress up and cruise Manhattan in his yellow Ferrari. Subtlety was not his thing.

But his longer track record was a much more understated affair – and as in clothes, so in music: Davis once explained that he had to keep changing, that it was his curse. Contrary to his culture and his race – and so speaking to his progressive spirit – he was a regular of Charlie Davidson's The Andover Shop in

Cambridge, Massachusetts. It was here where Ivy League style took hold, where the WASPish undergraduates of Harvard, Princeton or Columbia developed a relaxed style of dress that would arguably become the lynchpin for western male sartorial standards for the next half-century and more: crisp white button-down Oxford shirts and army surplus khakis, saddle shoes and penny loafers, hopsack blazers and flannel trousers, knitted and repp ties and shawl-collar cardigans.

It was, defiantly, the look of good grooming, privilege and money, and it was defiantly white – yet now worn by a man whose comments on race issues were often outspoken (at a White House reception in honour of Ray Charles in 1987, a society lady next to Davis asked him what he had done to be invited. 'I've changed music four or five times,' Davis replied. 'What have you done of any importance other than be white?').

Davis, in his dress, came to crystallize the jazz cool hipster style of individualistic, bohemian clothing that had developed during the 1950s, from Dizzy Gillespie's double-breasted pinstripes, goatee, black horn-rimmed glasses and beret to Lester Young's tilted pork-pie hat and Thelonius Monk's outsized specs. But it was Davis – searching for a look to announce his post-heroin, cleaned-up comeback – who made the clarion call to this definitive, artsy, jazz dress when, in 1954,

Giant sunglasses, giant shoulders, giant identity
bracelet – Davis photographed in 1969.

At the photo shoot for the *Miles in the Sky* album cover in 1968 – note the accessories: the bold scarf and the Breitling watch.

'TO KEEP CREATING YOU HAVE TO BE ABOUT CHANGE.'

Davis in more bohemian style, performing in 1970.

the aptly named jazz promoter Charles Bourgcois first took him to the blue-blood haberdasher to find what he would call Davis' 'costume'.

The trumpet player left having put the 'I' back into Ivy, with his own distinctive blend of preppy basics, most notably perhaps an enduring love of loafers, specifically Bass Weejuns. Indeed, in 1965, jazz critic George Frazier would dub Davis the 'Warlord of the Weejuns' in the liner notes for a greatest hits collection. His 'costume', as superficially conservative as it was then, was replete with detail: he would wear drop-shoulder sports jackets – they were easier to play trumpet in – without cuff-buttons or breast pocket, or formal, pinstriped double-breasted suits with more casual patch pockets; a knotted neckerchief under the button-down collar of his shirts, often with an unusual pullover placket. If others seemed to be aping his style, he shifted gear – on to a more slimline European suiting, for example.

Certainly Davis came as far stylistically as he did musically. When starting out he would scrimp to wear second-hand Brooks Brothers suits he would buy from pawn shops. These would prove a lesson in style: defending his choice to a disapproving Dexter Gordon, Davis pointed out that 'this

shit' had cost him a lot of money. 'The shit ain't hip,' Gordon retorted. 'See, it ain't got nothing to do with the money, it's got something to do with hipness.' Come 1960, *Down Beat* magazine was hailing Davis as a showcase of 'what the well-dressed man will wear next year'. In 1973, his style was still being celebrated – that year, *Esquire* named Davis as a model of style for his bespoke suits, made by Emsley in New York and costing him what was then a whopping $185 each.

His slick shifts were marked as inspirational. For one of his performances at the Newport Jazz Festival of 1967, Davis wore a black tuxedo with open-neck shirt – look closer though and the jacket has a tone-on-tone leopard print over it; yet for another he appeared in a custom-made, side-vented seersucker sack coat, club-collared shirt and a bow tie, on most other men the look of a door-to-door salesman. And yet Davis pulled each look off – the glamorous and the nerdish – with equal aplomb.

'For me,' Davis noted, 'music and life are all about style.' But not one easily emulated. 'I'm not advocating that all men aspire to dress like Davis,' Frazier wrote. 'That would be unrealistic, for it is this man's particular charm that [makes him] unique.'

'FOR ME,
MUSIC AND
LIFE ARE
ALL ABOUT
STYLE.'

Miles Davis outside Prestige Records office, 1950s, wearing a
penny collar and softly draping Brooks Brothers suit. By 1970 he
favoured a more structured but still statement suit, below.

Polka dots and checks – a subtle blend of pattern
from Davis at La Villette jazz festival, Paris, 1991.

Miles Davis surveys the endless array of his by
then more outlandish style, at home in LA, 1971.

MILES DAVIS

SAMMY DAVIS JR

1925 – 1990

Bling before bling – a bejewelled
Sammy Davis Jr in the 1960s.

'Sammy is particular,' reads the advertisement for clothing company Groshire Austin Leeds. 'He knows we don't manufacture suits. We make them ... When they ask Sammy about his Nehru suit, he tells them he had it made. And he's not putting them on.' Sammy Davis Jr – actor, dancer, singer, entertainer – was said to have owned some 200 Nehru suits, so many that by the late 1960s it had became something of a signature.

But this often self-described 'one-eyed Negro Jew' and, one might add, skinny and short to boot, standing just 5 feet 3 inches (1.6 metres), was more than his preference for collarless jackets. Indeed, the cornerstone of what was dubbed the 'Rat Pack' – the performing and style-shaping triumvirate of Davis, Frank Sinatra and Dean Martin – would also become the first African-American cover star of American *GQ* magazine, in 1967. It was a significant moment for a performer who had faced considerable racism – and done much to stand up to it –

throughout his career: 'Being a star has made it possible for me to get insulted in places where the average Negro could never hope to go and get insulted,' he quipped in his autobiography, *Yes I Can*. In a grey and black windowpane double-breasted suit, matching coat and Cuban heels – another of his favourites – Davis was, as the *GQ* cover put it simply, 'something else!'.

So too was his sense of style, reflecting shifts with the times – be that the skinny suits, slim ties, stovepipe trousers and cropped jackets of the mid 1950s and 1960s, or leather patchwork vests, jumpsuits and full-length fur coats of the 1970s – but always making it his own. While sometimes preppyish – in a one-button suit and button-down shirt – it was a preppyness he would undercut with a loosened tie and dandyish pocket square. And at other times – whether out of oversight or a sense of panache – he would break the rules, wearing, for example, a gold tie-bar conspicuously low down his tie, or plenty of gold jewellery even with black-tie formal attire. Such was

Davis wearing a turtleneck sweater and a Nehru
jacket – buttoned only at the bottom – in 1968.

Davis turns a touch hippy with decorated waistcoat, singing as host on *The Hollywood Palace* TV show, in 1969.

'WHAT HAVE
I GOT?
NO LOOKS,
NO MONEY,
NO EDUCATION.
JUST TALENT.'

Davis in 1960 wearing more conservative garb – but note the decorated buttons.

the diversity of his dress that Dean Martin once asked Frank Sinatra, while the three of them were on stage together, 'Hey! How come we wear trousers and he wears leotards?'.

Davis understood the impact of the right sartorial statement at the right time too – typically, for example, he would perform one of his greatest hits, 'Mr Bojangles', in a black derby hat, carrying a cane and using a gold-plated microphone. Offstage, as well as on, his image fitted the bill of a legendary carouser, having burned through more than $50 million in earnings to leave him almost destitute at the time of his death in 1990 – he gambled, drank and smoked to excess, such that cigarette smoke and a tumbler of whisky became accessories. After a spell of sobriety he joked that 'the hardest thing is waking up in the morning and realizing that's as good as you're going to feel all day'.

Davis in a black leather jacket and plenty of jewellery, in 1967.

SAMMY DAVIS JR

JAMES DEAN

1931 – 1955

James Dean in 1955 – his
collar in elegant disarray.

James Dean lived a short life, before his death aged 24 behind the wheel of his Porsche 550 Spyder, and made only a few films. But even by the time of the posthumous release of *Giant* in 1956, the trailer was calling him the 'star who became a legend, who spoke for the restless young as no one has before or since'. Dean spoke for all the 'restless young' – referring to the then new idea of the teenager, distinct in attitude and culture from their parents – as much sartorially as attitudinally.

On-screen, his style embodied a distinctly American look of the era, be that the western clothing of *Giant*, preppy in *East of Eden* or, most influentially, the jeans, white T-shirt and red blouson that he wore in *Rebel Without a Cause*. This latter look became the definition of teen style – although since the film was initially shot in monochrome before switching to colour after good test audience feedback, it almost didn't.

But, importantly to his wider influence, Dean dressed as though for a fashion plate in his personal life too, his dress also reflecting the pioneer spirit inherent to the hard-wearing, masculine clothing he preferred. He was, after all, keen on pursuits such as motorcycle riding and racing-car driving, but also no stranger to cleaning out the pigs on the Indiana farm of his aunt and uncle, who raised him after his mother's death when he was nine.

His clothing choices might include denims or work pants, patch-pocket work shirts, striped Oxfords, Bretons or T-shirts, motorcycle boots or Jack Purcell sneakers, Perfecto black-leather biker jacket, flight jacket or double-breasted overcoat, aviator sunglasses or horn-rimmed glasses and, capping the look, seemingly glued to his bottom lip, an ever-present cigarette. Shirts were invariably worn undone, collars crumpled or turned up. His quiff alone was instantly recognizable.

Such choices might seem anodyne in the twenty-first century, but in the 1950s they represented an unconventional, outsider style that previous generations might have considered scruffy and disrespectful, much as the older actors Dean worked with were said to resent his more fluid, instinctual 'method' approach to acting. His friend, actor Martin Landau, identified the importance of Dean's image: 'Jimmy represented something that was happening in the States after the Second World War. Until that moment in time, grown-ups – adults – set the styles for clothing, set the styles for music, set the styles for everything that was going on.' Not after Dean.

Even when a rising star, working in Hollywood and establishing his reputation as a good actor, Dean kept his tiny, fifth-floor New York apartment – just about big enough for a bed, desk and hotplate (with a shared bathroom down the

A stark, graphic silhouette – James Dean
in his greatcoat, in New York City, 1955.

James Dean in *Rebel Without a Cause*, 1955.

James Dean in 1955, posing with the Bloom Award he received for his role in the 1952 play *The Immoralist*. He died later that year.

A posed film publicity shot, an unusually besuited James Dean reading a script.

hallway). And, in respects, it, like the breakaway style with which he came to be associated, was also typically teenaged: messy, lined with books and records, with modern art reproductions pin-tacked to the walls.

Dean was famously, also, a man of very few words, which added to the mystique, the mythology, the cool, that rapidly built up around him during his brief career, and which only grew after his untimely end. And soon after – within weeks – the wreckage of his sports car was on display to paying customers. 'He was very afraid of being hurt,' was the assessment of

Elizabeth Taylor, his co-star in *Giant*. 'He was afraid of opening up in case it was turned around and used against him.'

One of the few things he would come to be widely quoted on was his opinion that dying in a racing-car crash could hardly be bettered as a way to end one's life. 'It's fast and clean and you go out in a blaze of glory.' Dean could not have known, of course, that in time he would come to be the poster boy for the 'live fast and die young' philosophy.

ALAIN DELON

b. 1935

Alain Delon wearing a suit and
sunglasses, on the set of the film
The Sicilian Clan, 1969.

Is it arrogance or self-assuredness that made Alain Delon such a magnetic screen presence through the history of French New Wave cinema? After all, the man once conceded that 'I like to be loved like I love myself'. 'The simple truth is that I am an enormous star all over the world. I like that because it enables me to live well,' he said on another occasion – despite this being somewhat short of the truth: although he had contracts and opportunity, he never did crack Hollywood.

Yet if – as in *Borsalino*, a gangster film named for the hat Delon wears in it – the actor was often set in counterpoise to that other style leader of the 1950s and 1960s, Jean-Paul Belmondo – the rough and reckless to Delon's smooth and brooding – then it was Delon who actually had the tough beginnings. Repeatedly expelled from school, he joined the French Navy as a paratrooper, seeing action in Indochina – and serving time for being undisciplined – then, after being dishonourably discharged, became a waiter, then a porter. Despite this, his classical looks and confidence – whether staged or real – saw him invariably cast in the mould of the well-to-

do, whether that might be the gallant officer of *The Leopard* or the usurping identity thief, affecting a class he didn't have, in *Plein Soleil*.

That film in particular was a benchmark in Delon's wider appreciation as more than a French archetype – all cool reserve and icy masculinity, all undone tie and bottom lip-sticking Gauloises. It connected him in the public consciousness with a style of louche, rich, free living of which the Côte d'Azur was then the epicentre. While the film wardrobe was not of his design – that was the work of costume designer Bella Clément – it did seal the actor's association with a certain monied chic then emulated by young men across the Continent. Delon was all traditional English weekend attire – an open-neck shirt and black rectangular sunglasses in summer, an artfully wrapped scarf and black rectangular sunglasses in winter – worn with Gallic laissez-faire insouciance.

The yachting scenes in *Plein Soleil*, for example, are a rolling catwalk of off-white jeans and suede snaffle loafers, rolled khakis and espadrilles, polos, floral cabana sets and blousy, linen shirts worn artfully half-untucked – always unbuttoned to at least

Alain Delon photographed at
Bois de Vincennes in 1959.

'THE SIMPLE TRUTH IS THAT I AM AN ENORMOUS STAR ALL OVER THE WORLD. I LIKE THAT BECAUSE IT ENABLES ME TO LIVE WELL.'

Delon filming *The Yellow Rolls-Royce* in Florence, 1964.

Alain Delon with his wife Nathalie and their son Anthony in Monte Carlo, August 1965 – no need for buttons.

Alain Delon in May 1958.

Alain Delon on the set of the gangster
film *Borsalino* in Marseille, 1969.

mid-chest; those amid Rome's and Naples' cafe society are all
muted grey, pale cream or blue shantung silk suits, worn with a
plain contrasting shirt or tie. Delon certainly capitalized on the
association with style that followed: through the 1960s he was
a regular at fashion shows, especially those of French designers
such as Pierre Cardin, and by 1978 he had launched his own
fragrance, following that with clothing and accessories lines (still
in business at the time of writing).

Indeed, while aspects of Delon's life off-screen read more
like a film script – from the multiple infidelities to even the
accusation of murder (in 1968 his bodyguard was found dead in
a dumpster) – he certainly knew how to play, and look, the part.
'People go to the movies to dream,' as he once pointed out, 'not
to see actors with faces like their plumber.'

ALAIN DELON

JOHNNY DEPP

b. 1963

Johnny Depp – with tattoos, jewellery,
beard – at a photocall for the film
Transcendence, Los Angeles, 2014.

When the Council of Fashion Designers of America thought to give their Fashion Icon Award to a man for the first time in 2012, the organization – which hosts the US fashion industry's equivalent of the Oscars – didn't have far to look. Johnny Depp's name had come up every year since the Fashion Icon Award was initiated. In an interview with *People* magazine, the CFDA's CEO put the reasoning thus: '[Depp] doesn't worry about what someone else is going to think. That's what we liked about him: he's got no fear and dresses for himself. You see pretty much every guy wearing a bracelet or two [now]. You look at Johnny and he's got 40 of them on and he's been doing that for a while.'

And those are not Depp's only favoured accessories: alongside his horn-rimmed, blue-tinted glasses (a matter of necessity, not style), he favours necklaces and rings ('my little trinkets', as the man who was signed in 2015 to be the face of Dior colognes has called them), and typically sports an Indiana Jones-style fedora in an era when formal, broad-brimmed hats are rarely worn. These are strange choices perhaps for a man who describes himself as 'shy ... not the most extrovert person in the world', but right for the man who has also claimed that 'everybody's weird. We should all celebrate our individuality and not be embarrassed or ashamed of it.' Many of his films are, indeed, a celebration of differences.

Certainly there is something of the quirky and bohemian in Depp's neo-grunge dress sense, and all the more so since the actor chooses to style what he wears with a touch of dishevelment: shirts are worn collars splayed and sleeves rolled or left undone at the cuff; waistcoats are rarely done all the way up; braces may hang low; a pocket watch chain may or may not have a pocket watch at the end of it; pockets themselves may be home to various bandanas or scarves; a suit – rarely worn with a tie – is likely to be in a vintage style, a three-piece pinstripe perhaps; fingernails may carry a bright hue of polish; boots, like his favoured leather jackets, are beaten up – much as the rest of his clothing might be worn ripped or holed. Indeed, if other stars seek to impress the paparazzi with a brand-new outfit for every public appearance, Depp's clothes make reappearances repeatedly over the years, ageing with him.

Johnny Depp promoting *The Tourist* in 2010 – note the multiple scarves and layered patterns and textures.

Johnny Depp in a Mister Freedom waistcoat – note the bandana tucked into his jeans pocket, and the belt buckle pulled to one side.

'I DON'T PRETEND TO BE CAPTAIN WEIRD. I JUST DO WHAT I DO.'

Fellow hat wearers – Johnny Depp and Keith Richards out and about in London, 2010.

It might be said that the western-meets-piratical style of Captain Jack Sparrow, the character Depp played in the *Pirates of the Caribbean* film franchise, is not that far from his own. But this is no costume for Depp – his style's appropriateness to the occasion is rarely a concern for him: the same personal aesthetic applies whether he is out for a Sunday walk or at a gala ball.

Not that Depp's style is as thrown together as it might at first seem. 'I love the idea of changing my look,' Depp said to *Interview* magazine. 'I always felt that if you're not trying something different each time out of the gate, you're being safe, and you don't ever want to find that place of safety.'

Depp affects a modern piratical style at the world premiere of
Pirates of the Caribbean: At World's End, in California, 2007.

JOHNNY DEPP

DUKE OF WINDSOR

1894 – 1972

Edward, Prince of Wales, in a rare early
colour photograph taken in 1930.

HRH The Prince of Wales, later King Edward VIII then
the Duke of Windsor, having abdicated in 1936, followed a
family tradition in dressing with distinction. It was, after all,
his grandfather, King Edward VII, who had – back when the
British royal family was an international touchstone of good
dressing – effectively invented the modern dinner suit as an
adaptation of the 'Cowes' mess-cum-smoking jacket he had also
created to wear aboard his yacht and at semi-formal occasions.
In turn, during the 1930s, the Prince of Wales would introduce
the double-breasted dinner jacket – in midnight blue rather
than black – worn with a soft-front evening shirt, bringing in a
more comfortable, unceremonious style.

Indeed, such was his interest in dress that Edward worried
that it would adversely affect his public image. 'Clothes do make
the prince, at least in the eyes of the people,' as he observed
in his diary. Yet, he added, what might be the cost of being
perceived as a 'glorified clothes-peg'? History would, as it were,
absolve him: in the late 1990s the then-managers of Italian
tailoring companies Brioni and Kiton bought a selection of
his wardrobe for US$773,000, such was the Prince's perceived
influence on shaping twentieth-century menswear.

Edward, as *Cloth & Clothes* had it in 1953, 'led many of
the styles that are currently still in fashion'. And small wonder,

perhaps, when his position, not to mention the controversy
of his choices in his personal life, made him a figure of global
prominence: 'I was in fact produced as a leader of fashion, with
the clothiers as my showmen and the world as my audience,' he
once commented.

Again breaking with royal propriety, in 1960 Edward even
wrote a treatise on style, *A Family Album*, in which he noted
his influence: he wore a suit in Rothesay Hunting tartan to a
dinner near his home in Antibes in the early 1950s and 'one of
our guests mentioned the fact to a friend in the men's fashion
trade, who immediately cabled the news to America. Within a
few months tartan had become a popular material for every sort
of masculine garment, from dinner jackets and cummerbunds to
swimming trunks and beach shorts.'

This was, after all, the man whose contribution to the
menswear canon included the now-unquestioned idea of
wearing brown shoes with a navy suit and turn-ups on formal
suits – both transgressions for which his father roundly
chastised him. Such was Edward's preference for turn-ups, in
fact, that when cloth rationing during World War II prohibited
them, he ordered his trousers through H. Harris, a tailor in New
York.

He favoured a four-in-hand tie knot – which may or

Edward in 1936, now King Edward VIII,
wearing a boldly checked flat cap.

The Duke and Duchess of Windsor at
their villa in Biarritz, France, in 1951.

An athletic King Edward VIII and his future wife,
Wallace Simpson, sightseeing near Split, in 1936.

may not actually have been his father's creation, but which
he certainly popularized (the so-called Windsor knot was an
American invention named after him, but which he didn't
wear). He wore berets and Fair Isle sweaters, then certainly
atypical choices. And long before preppy introduced the idea
to menswear, Edward was an exemplar in how to wear pastel
colour, tartans (though only those he had the official right to
wear), argyles, paisleys and bold checks. The latter he pulled off,
despite his relative shortness, in large part by having the waist
of his jackets cut higher than normal in order to accentuate the
length of his legs.

Through his patronage of Savile Row tailor Frederick
Scholte, the man who pioneered cutting suit cloth on the
bias, Edward also ushered in a much softer, more flexible
style of tailoring. This may have been in line with Edward's
own style dictum – 'dress soft' (he also favoured soft-collared
shirts) – but was sufficiently radical that, despite the boost
to business it would bring, tailors often refused to make suits
to his specification. One, for example, baulked at the idea of
fitting trousers with this newfangled contraption known as a
zip (Edward would happily wear elastic-waisted trousers too).
Edward usually had to have his then-favoured wide-legged
'Oxford bag'-style trousers tailored in the United States, since
none on Savile Row would break free of what he called 'English
trousers, to be worn with braces high above the waist'. Edward
did not like braces.

He was, in short, an individualist in a social milieu that,
had it retained any influence, would not abide breaking rank. As
Nicholas Lawford said of Edward during the 1930s, 'In a world
where men tend to look more and more alike, he seems more
than ever endowed with the capacity to look like no one else.'

Edward in 1925 – note the small tab collar, plain tie and patterned pocket square.

DUKE OF WINDSOR

The Duke of Windsor accompanied by his wife
during a hunting party at Alsace in 1951.

The Prince of Wales, with his brother the Duke of York and the Duke's children, the future queen Princess Elizabeth and Princess Margaret, in 1935.

'CLOTHES DO MAKE THE PRINCE, AT LEAST IN THE EYES OF THE PEOPLE.'

The Duke of Windsor in the grounds of Ednam Lodge, Sunningdale, in 1946 – wearing the 'Prince of Wales' check that Edward popularized.

DOUGLAS FAIRBANKS JR

1909 – 2000

Douglas Fairbanks Jr, posed
in a rakish beret, in 1930.

'I'm rather conservative about suits,' Douglas Fairbanks Jr opined in the August edition of *Vogue*, 1966. 'Being an actor, I plan my clothes rather more. No one in public life can afford to overstep. One has a responsibility, and before I get anything new, I brood about it, try it out on my wife and daughters, and perhaps on someone in the Club. Once the suit is settled, then the only thing is shoes and linen ...'

Fairbanks may have had a complex relationship with his hero-worshipped father – son of Douglas Fairbanks Sr, himself a swashbuckling screen star and film mogul – feeling forever in his shadow. But in matters of style the son outshone the father, as perhaps, the mountain of suits, jackets and ties available at an auction of his estate in 2011 suggested. At the age of 50, he was being cited in George Frazier's seminal 1960 essay 'The Art of Wearing Clothes', as one of the 50 best-dressed men in the United States.

Certainly Fairbanks was a classic matinee idol – Noël Coward's 'Mad About the Boy' was said to have been inspired by him, though Fairbanks always joked that he thought it was Gary Cooper – and looked the part during and well beyond his acting career. Fairbanks signatures included the boutonnière,

pencil moustache and the hair precisely parted, always to the left (having settled on that direction in his late twenties). He wore the appropriately formal clothing of the day, with his suits from London's Stovel & Mason, shirts from Turnbull & Asser, Sulka or Charvet.

But he did so with great consideration: among his rules of good dressing were that combining patterns and colours is a matter of achieving a contrast – 'with a striped suit I wouldn't wear a striped shirt'; that shirt, tie and suit should not all be of the same colour or scale of pattern; that one should never be 'self-conscious about combination. ... Better to have [tie and pocket handkerchief] related, or even entirely unrelated, so long as they don't look wrong together.'

And, it might be added, Fairbanks dressed so with a degree of frugality: he regularly had old suits re-tailored to have them more fitting of the times – a trouser leg or lapel narrowed, perhaps – and dipped into an extensive tie collection to find the right note of the contemporary too. 'I never buy ties because I have so many,' added the man whose romantic life – married to Joan Crawford, relationships with Marlene Dietrich and Gertrude Lawrence – ensured his print-worthiness in a pre-

Douglas Fairbanks Jr, during the 1940s.

Douglas Fairbanks Jr in 1926, before he grew the
famous swashbuckling Fairbanks moustache.

'BEING AN ACTOR, I PLAN MY CLOTHES RATHER MORE. NO ONE IN PUBLIC LIFE CAN AFFORD TO OVER-STEP. ONE HAS A RESPONSIBILITY.'

Joan Crawford pours Fairbanks
Jr a cup of tea, in 1929.

Fairbanks Jr poses in two-tone shoes – note
how dark shirt and light trousers also affect a
two-tone combination.

paparazzi age. 'The other day a man came up to me and said, "You're really right up to the minute, wearing a wide tie." I said, "No, I've had this one since 1932."'

Fairbanks was also pernickety about practicality: soon after the end of World War II – during which he was a naval officer and founder of the US military's elite Beach Jumpers, a forerunner of the Navy SEALs – he began to have shoes with elastic sides made by his shoemaker, Maxwell's, in London, and didn't look back. Loafers were, as they were for Cary Grant,

Fairbanks' other choice – easy to slip off while travelling in car or plane. But this was not to say comfort trumped panache: even dressed-down, Fairbanks' attire was more carefully composed than many. A paparazzi picture of him vacationing in Venice in 1958 illustrates the point – Fairbanks, *sans* the usual gentlemanly formal attire, wears a long-sleeved polo shirt, tucked into tapered white trousers, tightened at the waist (*pace* Fred Astaire, perhaps) by use of a necktie. He looks ready to swashbuckle.

DOUGLAS FAIRBANKS JR

WALT FRAZIER

b. 1945

Walt Frazier in one of his many colourful suits, in New York, 2011 – a signature of his TV appearances as a sports commentator.

It began as a form of therapy. Walt Frazier was not playing so well – he was a rookie point guard for the New York Knicks basketball team – so would allay his woes by going shopping for clothes. 'I would go out, buy clothes, go to my room, dress up, and look in the mirror and say, "Well, I ain't playing good but I still look good!"' he once explained in an interview for *GQ*.

It was a habit that the basketball player – who would find his form to become one of the best players of all time, inducted into the Basketball Hall of Fame in the mid 1980s – would embrace. Indeed, a pioneer of bling, he would dress to excess, walking the thin line between dandy and gaudy: bold colours and prints, apricot scarves, big hats; later, custom suits and coats in mink and raccoon and shoulder-to-ankle leather, shoes in ostrich, alligator, stingray ... He spent big on clothes – an estimated $10,000 of his $25,000 rookie's salary.

The desire to dress up had been there since his childhood, as poor as it was – one of nine children, the first NBA game Frazier attended was one he played in. 'My dad was a good

dresser. So I remember as a kid admiring his clothes, trying to wear them when he wasn't around,' he once recalled. 'Nobody had any money. But when you went to church, people look nice. When you went downtown, you were taught that you were not only representing your family but your race.'

All the same, now a minor public figure, it took nerve to push the boundaries of men's dress as he did. When he first wore a wide-brimmed, brown felt Borsalino hat in 1967, his rookie year, his teammates literally laughed at him. Good fortune had it that a few weeks later, the Warren Beatty film *Bonnie and Clyde* was released – about the notorious Depression-era bank robbers. And so his fellow players gave Frazier the gift of a nickname instead: they called him 'Clyde'. And a sartorial, almost cartoonish character was born. He would, as historian George Nelson titled his documentary on Frazier, 'Disdain the Mundane'. 'I have to entertain myself. I like combinations that people wouldn't think would go normally together,' Frazier explained to the *New York Times*.

Cape, medallion, broad-brimmed hat – Walt Frazier poses
for a portrait at Madison Square Garden in New York, 1970.

Walt Frazier of the New York Knicks models a black mink fur coat
outside Manhattan's Plaza Hotel in New York, 1974.

Frazier owned a $20,000 Rolls-Royce but still took the subway to
work in New York, 1974 – he didn't like the city's congestion.

'I HAVE TO ENTERTAIN MYSELF.
I LIKE COMBINATIONS THAT
PEOPLE WOULDN'T THINK WOULD
GO NORMALLY TOGETHER.'

The nickname was a licence for Frazier to ditch the Brooks Brothers preppy style he had worn in his younger days, and to embrace his own outlandish creations, to see snazzy clothing – for which his 6-foot 4-inch (1.93-metre) baller's frame was ideally suited – as a signature, to remodel himself as the sport's style icon. 'After the game we're on the bus, and all the kids would go, "Clyde, c'mon, man, where's the mink? Clyde, c'mon, man, we wanted to see you dressed up!",' he has said. 'That's when I realized that people were really into the way I was dressing. So that's when I went somewhere I made sure I was dressed up.'

His sense of style was one Frazier developed with New York tailor Mohan Ramchandani, a man who knew next to nothing about basketball (he had no idea who Frazier was when he first entered his shop) but who could provide a show-stopping array of outlandish fabrics. 'Show me something that nobody else would wear,' was Frazier's challenge to the tailor. And sometimes that was too outlandish even for him. One

of his best-known jackets, a brown and cream cowhide – best known because, some years after retirement, he would become a staple basketball pundit on TV – was actually part of a suit. 'I thought it was going to be too much [together],' he noted.

The nickname and clothes habit also helped lead to a more lucrative licence. Basketball players of the 1970s were used to getting free sneakers to play in, but in 1973 Frazier became the first to be paid, $5,000 initially, to wear a certain style – Puma had an unusual suede model which, on signing Frazier, it promptly renamed the Clyde. It would prove to be a sneaker classic, selling well for decades after and supplementing a basketball career during which he made (by later standards) a paltry $3 million.

In 1974, Frazier would, with Ira Berkow, co-author what would become the bible on his distinctive style and attitude – *Rockin' Steady: A Guide to Basketball & Cool*. Its one clear message is summed up in Frazier's dictum: 'When you look good, you feel good. And when you feel good, you look good.'

WALT FRAZIER

SERGE GAINSBOURG

1928 – 1991

A cigarette was the only prop required –
Gainsbourg in Paris in 1966.

The idea that the necessity of being handsome precedes being stylish was not a notion Serge Gainsbourg agreed with. 'Ugliness is in a way superior to beauty because it lasts,' the poet and singer/songwriter of the 1960s and early 1970s French New Wave once put it. Not that that in any way prevented him from finding bedfellows: he notoriously had an affair with a married Brigitte Bardot. And sexuality – as his best-known heavy-breathing records 'Bonnie et Clyde' and 'Je t'aime … moi non plus' attest to – was his métier. So steamy was the latter song that Bardot pleaded with him not to release it; Gainsbourg didn't do so for almost two decades – perhaps because Bardot's marriage collapsed soon after – choosing to soon re-record it with his lover Jane Birkin. The Vatican banned it; a cheeky Gainsbourg appealed, citing the song's 'almost liturgical' melody. Later he would burn a 500-franc note on television in a protest against taxation and in 1975 would record *Rock Around the Bunker*, a concept album about the Nazis. For 1984's *Love on the Beat*, he sang about incest and dressed in drag for the cover.

Indeed, Gainsbourg lived with a certain roguish, sometimes boorish recklessness, drinking and smoking to excess – the permanent cigarette was in large part what underscored his French persona internationally, this enhanced by his giving himself the name Serge (he was born Lucien, 'a loser's name',

as he put it). Perhaps this is why he suffered a heart attack at just 45 years old. But, concerned with appearances and luxury comforts alike, he still insisted that he take his Hermès blanket with him in the ambulance, as well as two cartons of Gitanes. 'I had a heart attack. It proves that I have a heart,' quipped Gainsbourg, at once French national treasure and outsider.

And as in lifestyle, so in his style – said to be inspired by Salvador Dalí. By conventional standards, Gainsbourg was a scruffy dresser, pulling off an artful déshabillé with aplomb, albeit while never wearing the hippy clothing of the era either. He was rarely clean-shaven – Birkin had encouraged him to keep three days of stubble – and he had the kind of hairstyle that gave the impression, perhaps accurately, that he had just got out of bed in a hurry, having failed to look at his favoured Breitling Navitimer. His modish suits were typically dark and tight-fitting, perhaps worn with a crumpled collarless shirt and pointed boots or loafers. A leather jacket might be thrown over a tailored dress shirt, worn undone, the collar awry – again, affecting the image that he had literally thrown on whatever was to hand.

But he also had an eye for quirky touches of louche styling: he might, for example, wear pinstriped, two-piece tailoring with white Zizi Homme Repetto jazz shoes. He is said to have had

Power couple – Gainsbourg with Jane Birkin
wearing matching Cerruti creations at their
apartment in Paris, 1969.

Serge Gainsbourg in 1971, his tie and collar loosened.

Serge Gainsbourg posing for French sculptor Daniel Druet for the making of Gainsbourg's bust, 1981.

Dishevelment as style – Gainsbourg in 1980.

'MY MOTHER WAS BEAUTIFUL, MY FATHER TOO. I DO NOT SEE WHERE MY UGLINESS CAME FROM ... MAYBE FROM MY DOG.'

Gainsbourg and Bambou (his wife from 1981 until his death in 1991) on a TV set in Paris, in 1982. Gainsbourg wears one of the multiple pairs of jazz dance shoes that would become a signature.

sensitive feet and insisted his footwear be comfortable first and foremost; Birkin bought him his first pair and he is said to have gone through 30 pairs every year (they weren't made for wear outdoors) until his death in 1991. What's more, he might wear these without socks, this long before the idea of dispensing with socks became fashionable. A peak-lapel blazer would be worn over a white T-shirt, with jeans – again, a progressive look for the period. When he wore a denim jacket it was worn undone – and over nothing at all. And he was not above looking positively space age at times: at home he and Birkin wore matching Cerruti silver mail-effect tops.

When Gainsbourg died, the French culture minister Jack Lang said that the songwriter had personified 'a certain ideal of freedom'. His libertine style, both in manner and dress, however, had come at some cost. As Gainsbourg put it, with typical wit: 'I've succeeded at everything except my life.'

CARY GRANT

1904 – 1986

Sharp suited, hair parted, Cary Grant
in 1933, and smoking a cigarette
outdoors in 1934, opposite.

'I'm often asked for advice or an opinion about clothes ... but I'm not inclined to regard myself as an authority on the subject. Many times during my years in films, some well-meaning group has selected me as best-dressed man of the year, but I've never understood why. The odd distinction surprises me: first, because I don't consider myself especially well dressed, and, secondly, I've never, as far as I can compare the efforts of others with my own, gone to any special trouble to acquire clothes that could be regarded as noticeably fashionable.'

So said the actor Cary Grant in an interview with *This Week* magazine around 1962. Grant – so often held up as the ultimate exemplar of the immaculately attired male – seemed genuinely bemused by the idea of his style influence. In the same interview, he further commented how some of his slimline, typically sober suits were a decade or two old, that many were ready-made, that those that weren't were not the work of any one special tailor – he shopped with Dunhill and with Savile Row's Kilgour, French & Stanbury in London and Schiaparelli in Paris, but also had those suits copied in Hong Kong. Some were battered by work – like many actors at the time, he was often filmed wearing his own suits, such as the mid-grey worsted wool suit worn for *North by Northwest*. In the end, six were required just to get through the crop-spraying scene.

And, here, after all, was a man all too conscious of the gulf between his public and private personae: 'Everyone wants to be Cary Grant. Even I want to be Cary Grant,' once noted the man born Archibald Leach, whose troubled upbringing – estranged from his father, led to believe his mentally ill mother was dead – inspired his sense of self-creation. 'I pretended to be somebody I wanted to be and I finally became that person. Or he became me. Or we met at some point,' said Grant. 'I tried to copy men I thought were sophisticated – like Douglas Fairbanks [who happened to be on the same ship Grant emigrated from the UK to the United States aboard] or Cole Porter ...' Even his stage name was, it is said, chosen because the initials echoed those of similarly dapper Gary Cooper and Clark Gable.

But, for all that role-play, Grant's figure – 6 foot 1 inch (1.68 metres), lithe and, since he started out in show business as a vaudevillian acrobat, athletic – made him well suited to whatever he put on. It gave him a presence that saw him in the running to play the first cinematic James Bond but which worked just as well in thrillers – *To Catch a Thief* – and romantic comedy – *That Touch of Mink*, to cite two of his more style-centric films. And, what's more, he understood clothing – during the 1930s he was a silent partner in a menswear store on Los Angeles' Wilshire Boulevard, Neale's Smart Men's Apparel.

Grant's mid-grey worsted wool suit
and plain tie made famous by the
'advertising man, not a red herring'
in *North by North West*, 1959.

Cary Grant, sockless in loafers, for *That Touch of Mink*, 1962.

He even worked in the store when not wanted on set. Marlene Dietrich, a co-star at the time, subsequently referred to him as 'the shirt salesman'.

And Grant did offer some insight as to why he might, then as now, have been so highly praised for his attire. First, that 'it isn't only money that determines how well a man dresses – it's personal taste'. And second, that it pays to avoid the extremes: all of his suits, Grant said, were 'in the middle of fashion ... not far out, nor overly conservative ... I've worn clothes of extreme style but only in order to dress appropriately for the type of character I played ... Otherwise, simplicity, to me, has always been the essence of good taste. ... The most reliable style is in the middle of the road – a thoughtful sensible position in any human behaviour.'

This last piece of advice was, indeed, the sort of witticism that serves to underline how Grant was widely considered the essence of debonair (don't wear huge, flashy cufflinks, he also recommended – 'they are not only ostentatious but a menace to the enamel on your car and your girlfriend's eye'). But it also fits well with the image of the screen star – nonchalant, graceful, unhurried, his own man. 'Wear, not only your clothes, but yourself, well, with confidence,' he would say. Or, as his father had taught him, partly in approbation of his son's youthful preference for loud socks, 'remember, that's you walking down the street, not the socks'.

Cary Grant posed in a trilby hat for a publicity shot, in 1947.
Grant was rarely photographed in a hat otherwise.

CARY GRANT

Cary Grant in 1940.

'WEAR, NOT ONLY
YOUR CLOTHES,
BUT YOURSELF,
WELL, WITH
CONFIDENCE.'

Style generations – Cary Grant shares a beer with Paul
Newman and his wife Joanne Woodward, in 1965.

Grant – again sockless in loafers – reads through a script in 1955.

CARY GRANT

JIMI HENDRIX

1942 – 1970

Jimi Hendrix, in balloon sleeves and
full psychedelic style, playing the Royal
Albert Hall, London.

The opulence of Jimi Hendrix's style can hardly be topped: lush velvet, embroidery, billowing fabrics, clashing prints and bold colour – purple above all; adorning tight, flared trousers, waistcoats, stack-heeled boots, fringed jackets, bead necklaces, medallions, multiple rings, scarves and wide-brimmed hats, themselves decorated with brooches and bandanas. It was, as Jim Morrison's dress was too, a template for rock style. And amid this excess there was room for the quirky – for a while, for instance, Hendrix would wear scarves tied around one arm and one leg. Even for the 1960s period – when a hippy sensibility was transforming the way young men were dressing, underpinning a new sartorial distinction between generations – Hendrix's brash style stood out, exemplary of the counterculture and his psychedelic sounds alike.

Not that Hendrix had always dressed this way – playing backing guitar as a younger man on the US R & B circuit, he wore a dark suit. But the desire to up the ante was there: during the early 1960s Hendrix played with the likes of Sam Cooke, Ike and Tina Turner and Little Richard – and he left Richard's company to form his own band after the singer instructed him to tone down his garb; Hendrix was drawing too much attention away from him.

A trip to London in 1966 – when the guitarist was looking to launch his career as a solo act, taking with him among his few possessions a set of hair curlers – only helped reinforce Hendrix's break with this sober style: he was a regular at the seminal clothes stores I Was Lord Kitchener's Valet and Granny Takes a Trip – which also drew artists such as The Beatles and The Rolling Stones; indeed, the hand-painted silk jacket Hendrix wore when he burned his guitar at the 1967 Monterey Pop Festival was designed by Chris Jagger, Mick's brother. It was at these new stores where he bought an ornate, nineteenth-century braided British Hussar jacket that would become a favourite. It also attracted the wrong kind of attention: British veterans often told him he hadn't earned the right to wear it. Hendrix would reply with a reminder that he had, at least, served in the US Army's 101st Airborne Division.

One anecdote catches just how excessive Hendrix's style may have been perceived (or perhaps how dry Liverpudlian wit can be): Hendrix and fellow band member Noel Redding went to a Liverpool pub between sets, only to have the bartender refuse to serve them. Hendrix asked the bartender if it was because he is black. 'It has nothing to do with your race,' replied the bartender. 'We do not want your kind in here. The sign

Jimi Hendrix photographed among smoke and flames
for his album *Electric Ladyland*, London, 1968.

Jimi Hendrix with Noel Redding (bass) and
Mitch Mitchell (drums) in the 1960s.

'YOU HAVE TO
GO ON AND
BE CRAZY.
CRAZINESS IS
LIKE HEAVEN.'

A still from the film *Woodstock* in 1970 – outlandish fringes
were a staple of Hendrix's stage clothing.

Jimi Hendrix in nineteenth-century Hussar jacket, at Monterey Pop Festival, 1967 – taken the day of his debut performance in the United States.

Hendrix in 1967 – clashing colour and pattern under a customized vintage military jacket.

outside is clear about it.' Hendrix and Redding went outside. The sign said 'Clowns will not be served'. The city was hosting a clown convention that week.

In 1968, Hendrix's style was given more consideration with the hiring of Michael Braun and Toni Ackerman, who worked as the designers of his clothing until Hendrix died in 1970. The duo created the jacket Hendrix wore at Woodstock, as well as shirts with 'witch sleeves' so wide as to almost touch the floor. 'It was the perfect storm,' Braun told the *Tampa Tribune* in 2014, (he also would design for Aerosmith and Bob Dylan). 'Two crazy people making crazy clothes for a guy who was crazy

enough to wear them.'

When Hendrix couldn't meet Braun and Ackerman to discuss clothes, he would occasionally place an order by postcard: 'Please don't use stiff material for the pants,' reads one. 'Try working in stones and jewellery in vests and pants ... More shirts with odd sleeves, very soft material,' and fasten these with what Hendrix calls 'sticky type buttons', also known as Velcro.

DAVID HOCKNEY

b. 1937

David Hockney, in his signature
round-framed spectacles, on the set
of *Ubu Roi* at the Royal Court Theatre,
London, 1996.

One might expect as bold a colourist as artist David Hockney to make colour a major aspect of his wardrobe – and that he has certainly done. The most vibrant hues, many of them far from being normal in the male wardrobe – for instance, pinks, yellows and reds, as well as softer pastels – have always been as much a part of Hockney's personal style as the signature, black, graphic outsized spectacles of his younger days. 'I prefer living in colour,' as the artist put it.

But there was never a sense that this was anything more than a continuation of the way he saw the world – especially that of sun-drenched life in 'visually stunning' Los Angeles, which informed many of his more famous 'swimming pool' works – into the way he dressed. Even a grey suit would not be left without an under-layer of some bright shade. Indeed, what makes Hockney distinctive in his appearance is his attire's seeming very lack of consideration, its seeming spontaneity (even if he once noted that 'you must plan to be spontaneous'). Although he resents being lumped together with the pop artists of the 1960s, he was friends with Andy Warhol, an explorer of the power of public image.

Sometimes Hockney's spontaneity was more literally true: his almost bleach-blonde bowl-cut hair for example, always messy, was said to have been retained after he and a group of friends immediately decided to dye their hair after seeing a TV ad for Clairol during the 1960s that proclaimed 'blondes have more fun'. Other times it was more suggested: Hockney's style is defined by its very thrown-together, loose-fit, defiantly un-pressed aesthetic, especially in his preference for wide-legged trousers, baggy cable-knit sweaters and crumpled trench coats; or his predilection for mismatching, be that a clash of colour – Hockney is not above wearing odd socks, either by accident or design, or of teaming a striped rugby shirt with yellow trousers and battered, grubby pumps, as he often was photographed wearing during the 1970s – or of pattern – a polka-dot scarf worn with a checked cap, for example, or Breton and patterned braces.

Indeed, a key element of Hockney's English gentlemanly style has always been his regard for striking accessories, often wearing many at once – pocket square, floppy bow or loosened knitted tie, bucket or newsboy hat, cricket cap, suede shoes,

David Hockney, photographed
by Cecil Beaton, in 1970.

Hockney, in front of his 1968 painting *Hotel L'Arbois*.

David Hockney in 1971 – wearing rugby
shirt, olive-green trousers and that
shock of bleach-blond hair.

'THE IDEA OF THE RIGID STYLE SEEMED TO ME THEN SOMETHING YOU NEEDN'T CONCERN YOURSELF WITH. IT WOULD TRAP YOU.'

Hockney poses for a photo shoot in
1995 – easy and unstructured, his style is
nevertheless carefully considered.

boutonnière. 'Style,' he once said, 'is something you can use, and you can be like a magpie, just taking what you want. The idea of the rigid style seemed to me then something you needn't concern yourself with. It would trap you.'

But then individuality has always been important to Hockney: even as a teenager in the northern working-class British city of Bradford, he would dress with a dandy style of his own making. The fashion designer Celia Birtwell may have become his muse, but that same boy could hardly have imagined that, decades later, he would have a Vivienne Westwood jacket named after him, or be cited as the inspiration for an entire collection from Burberry.

DAVID HOCKNEY

JOHN F. KENNEDY

1917 – 1963

President John F. Kennedy with cigar
and a copy of the *New York Times*
aboard the *Honey Fitz* in 1963.

John F. Kennedy, 35th President of the United States, was not persuaded. Representatives of the American hat-making industry wrote to him pleading for him to wear one – his refusal to do so was killing business, such was the young, handsome president's standing as a role model of style.

Yes, other presidents before had become known for their sartorial quirks – Dwight Eisenhower's cropped military jackets, for example, or Harry Truman's Hawaiian shirts. But Kennedy defined dress for his generation. And he saw hats as belonging to that of his father. Even during his inauguration, in white tie, he mostly carried his top hat. Rarely did it cover the tousled mop of hair that both framed his youth and, what is more, helped make a politician a pin-up for the nation's women. As *GQ* magazine noted in 1961, 'Cigar sales have soared (Jack smokes them). Hat sales have fallen (Jack does not wear them). Dark suits, well-shined shoes, avoid button-down shirts (Jack says they are out of style).'

Of course, Kennedy had been introduced to the idea of the importance of being well dressed when just a small boy. As the son of Joe Kennedy, United States Ambassador to the United Kingdom, he had to represent both his family and nation abroad. Living in London introduced him to Savile Row tailoring too. Yet although the style he would come to embody

was of his privileged, wealthy class – Kennedy's east coast, Ivy League preppy dressing was quintessentially American – in his simple, clean, casual, perhaps European-inflected interpretation, it reflected a break with the past.

If the American male of the 1950s wore boxy, wider-shouldered, built-up double-breasted suits, Kennedy proposed the elegance of slim, lightly padded, dark navy or grey single-breasted, two-button suits – both buttons of which, contrary to dress etiquette, he would typically wear fastened – worn with with turned-up, flat-fronted, slimline trousers, teamed with a white cutaway collar, monogrammed shirt and dark, narrow tie, perhaps with an understated pattern or a regimental stripe.

Accessories were few: just a hint of white handkerchief in his breast pocket, a gold Omega Ultra Thin watch, gold oval cufflinks carrying the seal of the president. Even for appearances in sub-zero temperatures, he shunned the wearing of a heavy overcoat, as if it would diminish the power of his starkly direct, newly athletic image.

Kennedy was protective of this image too. Although a Brooks Brothers regular (he presented monogrammed Brooks Brothers umbrellas to his groomsmen on his wedding day), he had his custom tailor too: the New York's outpost of Savile Row's H. Harris. Until, that is, proprietor Sam Harris revealed

A portrait of Senator Kennedy – and
future US President – in 1954.

Brothers John, Robert, and Edward Kennedy are pictured in Hyannisport, Massachusetts, 1960 – each wears the easy preppy style that defined their class.

Kennedy during the presidential campaign, 1960.

to *Life* magazine that the commander-in-chief was a client. Kennedy duly switched to Chipp, the tailor too for brother Bobby and brother-in-law Peter Lawford.

Kennedy's image, after all, mattered – and he knew it. This was a modern style for the first televisual president – some 9 per cent of US households had a TV in 1950, up to some 90 per cent just ten years later; one who, as a candidate, would see off Richard Nixon in the first televised presidential debates at least in part because the latter could not disguise his permanent five o'clock shadow next to Kennedy's clean-cut freshness. Kennedy's was also a style, as Norman Mailer noted in his essay 'Superman Comes to the Supermarket', for the first president as product.

Certainly even before Kennedy became president in 1961, the media was fascinated by his seemingly fresh glamour. The same year, *Life* magazine wanted to show the Kennedy style

even while he was on vacation, typically sailing *Victura*, the boat gifted to him on his fifteenth birthday by his father: the polo shirts and cashmere sweaters, the deck shoes, khakis and – from his US Navy days – the G-1 military flight jacket. This was a president enigmatic in tortoiseshell sunglasses carefully selected from makers such as American Optical, Universal Optical or Titmus.

Indeed, it was a contemporary style being observed and commented on years earlier. In 1958, the *New York Times* was trumpeting the fact that, during one speech, 'Jack Kennedy – the young eastern millionaire with the Harvard accent, the Brooks Brothers couture and the egghead ideas – had them standing on their chairs, whistling and shouting.' And he would not stop there.

Kennedy – in flight jacket, khakis and sneakers – with his brother-in-law
Peter Lawford aboard the United States Coast Guard yacht *Manitou*, 1962.

JOHN F. KENNEDY

JACK KEROUAC

1922 – 1969

The cover of Jack Kerouac's 1959
spoken-word LP *Blues and Haikus*
(with Al Cohn and Zoot Sims).

In an era in which intellectuals and artists would more typically aspire to wear a suit – to move up in the world socially and, as it followed then, sartorially – Jack Kerouac went the other way. While he was typically photographed in blazer and tie for official publicity stills, in his personal life he dressed out of solidarity with the working man, like a working man – that of the world, indeed, into which he was born.

This meant less of the all-black, Frenchified ensembles the 'beat generation' is often perceived as wearing in the popular imagination, and more of the rugged, practical and affordable sportswear and military surplus from the depots that had sprung up across the United States to offload the glut of servicemen's clothing after World War II: tight black or white T-shirts (designed as underwear), plaid work shirts and PT sweatshirts (Kerouac was a star college athlete), standard-issue khakis and, later, jeans, cowboy or work boots, horsehide leather bomber jackets and US Navy pea coats (he was also in the Navy for two weeks before being honourably discharged).

On him, a celebrity novelist and a leading figure in a new wave of pioneering literary stylists, such clothes had resonance: he once wore black jeans and a red-and-black-checked shirt to sit on a public discussion panel of intellectuals. Everyone

else dressed with the respectable conservatism that would be expected of them. Such attire also ensured he stood apart from his beat contemporaries, the likes of William Burroughs, whose more upper-class background led him to wear a three-piece suit, or Allen Ginsberg, whose style became increasingly influenced by traditional eastern dress. Ginsberg, indeed, was happy to remove all of his clothes on stage while giving poetry readings. It was an attempt to get back to what he would call the 'naked original'.

But, like him, Kerouac's desire to see his wardrobe as utilitarian and fundamental – it was minimal in the sense that he simply didn't have many clothes – was also an attempt to somehow escape or disavow them, and the codes and the materialism they represented. Dean Moriarty, the main character in Kerouac's *On the Road* speaks of 'disemburdening' oneself of clothing.

Certainly, given that the 1950s saw, in the United States at least, the birth of modern consumerism, not bothering about the way he dressed was a means for Kerouac to make a statement, perhaps all the more so for a man who was far more deeply conservative in attitudes than is often believed. His clothes – invariably thrown on, crumpled and showing signs of hard

Allen Ginsberg's photo of Jack Kerouac on an apartment's fire escape in New York's Lower East Side, 1953. Kerouac is in his typical working-men's garb.

Neal Cassady and a sweatshirted Jack Kerouac in 1952.

A lumberjack of words – using a manual typewriter in a New York City loft, Kerouac produced the original manuscript of *On the Road* on a scroll during a three-week period in the spring of 1951.

Kerouac – in military surplus khakis and button-down shirt – outside the Kettle of Fish bar, Greenwich Village, 1958.

'GREAT THINGS ARE NOT ACCOMPLISHED BY THOSE WHO YIELD TO TRENDS AND FADS AND POPULAR OPINION.'

wear – were a counter to the new idea of the pristine, snappily attired youth. They also mirrored the other, similarly free-form new arts that Kerouac so loved: bebop, jazz, action painting and automatic writing.

Ironically, perhaps, Kerouac's freedom from concern about the way he was dressed in time made him appear effortlessly cool, inspiring emulation. Perceptions of hip – to use the terminology of Kerouac's circle, as it defined this new, creative lifestyle of the loose and easy – would henceforth be formed on the street and filter up, not trickle down from further up the social ladder.

Add heavy horn-rimmed glasses, and Kerouac's style would even become the new, lasting template for how the artist might be generally perceived – as an outsider and rebel, operating on the margins of society, free from social norms and dressing accordingly. Kerouac's style – and that of many disaffected men of his generation – may in itself have been basic and unconsidered, but its influence was revolutionary.

JACK KEROUAC

JEAN RENÉ LACOSTE

1904 – 1996

René Lacoste smiles after winning
the Gentleman's Singles Final against
Henri Cochet at Wimbledon in 1928 – a
heavy wool sweater was what one
wore while cooling down.

Jean René Lacoste was a tennis champion – winner of seven Grand Slam singles titles. But he was also a champion of a new kind of on-court style. Indeed, while the player clearly had an inventive and entrepreneurial streak – he would create the first steel tennis racquet and the first shock dampener – he also had a strong sartorial one.

If, pre-Lacoste, tennis was played in starched, full-sleeved shirts, young René had ideas for an alternative. He had seen his friend the Marquis of Cholmondeley wear a polo shirt – for playing polo in – to play a recreational game of tennis. And the benefits seemed immediately obvious. Lacoste had an English tailor make up a few samples to his own design, some in wool, others in a lightweight, breathable cotton known as 'jersey petit piqué'. Lacoste himself first wore one in 1926 at the US Open, and it caused a sensation – as well as planting the seed of what would become a menswear staple worn globally for decades to follow. 'Without style,' Lacoste noted, 'playing and winning are not enough.'

The design itself was smart in every sense. It had a soft ribbed collar, to prevent chaffing, but one stiff enough that it could be worn either turned up to protect the back of the neck – and it was certainly left visible by Lacoste when he donned his navy sweater to keep warm at the end of a match – or worn turned down without crumpling. Lacoste typically preferred to wear his done up to the neck. It had a 'tennis tail' – the shirt longer at the back to stay tucked in while serving. The elastic ribbing on the sleeves kept them in place.

And it was pioneering in other ways too: while offcourt Lacoste dressed in the personally tailored fashions of the day, preferring high-cut suits, sumptuous coats and co-respondent shoes, his tennis shirt presaged a fashion revolution in being one of the earliest garments to put a brand logo on the outside. The logo – drawn by artist Robert George – was, naturally, that deadly reptile, a version of the outsized badge Lacoste had, outlandishly perhaps, been wearing on his blazer since 1927 in honour of '*le Crocodile*'. This was the nickname Lacoste had been accorded after winning a set of alligator cases in a bet with the captain of the French Davis Cup team.

After Lacoste joined forces with knitwear manufacturing entrepreneur André Gillier in 1933, the Lacoste shirt – known

Renè Lacoste was nicknamed the Crocodile –
here he wears the badge on a polo shirt, 1938.

Lacoste wearing the crocodile
badge, 1937.

Lacoste in action in 1928 – in the shirt, trousers
and cap that gentleman players wore at the time.

Lacoste photographed in 1996 – still wearing
the polo shirt that took his name.

to the fledgling company as the 12-12 – went into production, initially available only in white, with colours not introduced until 1951. During the 1940s, another dapper tennis player, Fred Perry, introduced his own piqué shirt line (as well as co-inventing the sweatband with Austrian footballer Tibby Wegner).

Lacoste himself, however, remained baffled as to the appeal of what would become his shirt's famed badge: 'There are kinds of things that just don't have any good explanation,' he once said. 'I suppose you could say that if it had been a really nice animal, something sympathetic, then maybe nothing would have happened. Suppose I had picked a rooster. Well, that's French, but it doesn't have the same impact.'

'I SUPPOSE YOU COULD SAY THAT IF IT HAD BEEN A REALLY NICE ANIMAL, SOMETHING SYMPATHETIC, THEN MAYBE NOTHING WOULD HAVE HAPPENED. SUPPOSE I HAD PICKED A ROOSTER. WELL, THAT'S FRENCH, BUT IT DOESN'T HAVE THE SAME IMPACT.'

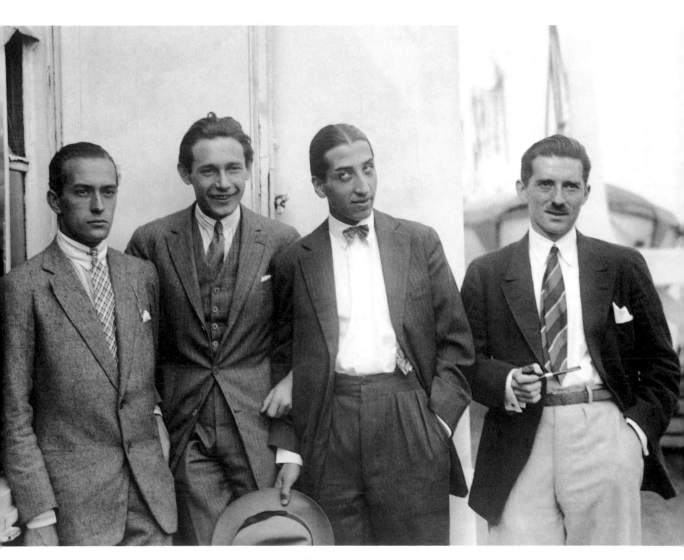

French tennis stars on board SS *France* in 1937. Left to right: Henri Cochet, Jean Borotra, René Lacoste – in petite bow tie – and Jacques Brugnon.

JEAN RENÉ LACOSTE

RALPH LAUREN

b. 1939

Ralph Lauren arrives at the 2005 Council
of Fashion Designers of America
Awards – breaking the rules by wearing
black tie only from the waist up.

A game changer in twentieth-century fashion, and the pioneer of arguably the era's definitive fashion company, Ralph Lauren once noted that the clothes he makes are, stylistically, the clothes he wears. 'I live different lives,' he noted in *The Telegraph*. 'You wear different clothes in each environment ... Jamaica has the sun, and the beach, and is very colonial. My ranch out west is very cowboy, and that's another dimension in my life. And the house on the beach in Montauk is very rustic. ... But my product and myself, it's the same thing. Anti-fashion fashion, whatever you want to call it, but something that's meant to be timeless. Watch Cary Grant in *To Catch a Thief* tomorrow, next year, whenever – you would still want to be him at the end of it. That's timeless.'

Lauren's own take on men's style – a romantic, historic, almost fantasy blend of WASPish Americana and traditional English, pre-war dress of a kind that, on first visiting England in the 1970s, he was sorely disappointed to discover had long been dismissed as fuddy-duddy – sees him run the gamut of the dressing-up box. Lauren has been snapped in styles from tweed jacket and jeans to tasselled leather trousers and neckerchief, from jodhpurs and riding boots to wide-lapelled, double-breasted suit to white dinner tuxedo, or – something of a signature – black tie with cowboy boots. These are nods to bygone stylistic worlds, or perhaps to worlds that never really existed in such perfect, untarnished form.

The period feel of his chameleon-like personal style – and, as he once noted, 'style is very personal – it has nothing to do with fashion' – has been reflected in his costume design work too, most memorably for *The Great Gatsby*. And on his own cinematic style heroes (Cary Grant, of course, but also Douglas Fairbanks Jr and Frank Sinatra): 'I was enamoured with the heroes I saw in films,' he has said. 'I always respected the type of man that made his mark on the world and, for me, the clothes and the identity of these men were inseparable.'

But Lauren's style developed young, before he'd ever gone to the movies. One of his earliest memories was looking through

Ralph Lauren at his Milan
showroom in 2002.

Ralph Lauren in 2010.

'SO WHAT I BELIEVE IN IS THIS TIMELESSNESS OF SOME OF THESE THINGS. THE TIMELESSNESS OF AN ATTITUDE.THE TIMELESSNESS OF AN OLD TWEED JACKET AND SUEDE ELBOW PATCHES.'

Ralph Lauren in 1996, ever the stylist whether dressed up or down.

a shop window at a pair of blue suede shoes – 'every pair of shoes I ever desired' as Lauren once called them – and as a teenager, when he couldn't find a replacement for his favourite, by then tattered Levi's western shirt, he made his own. His first proper job, in 1964, was as a tie salesman for Rivetz. 'I had no credentials but I dressed well,' he has said. He had ideas too – when, in 1967, his employer rejected ideas he had for three-and-a-half-inch-wide, richly woven tie designs, he had them made by Sulka and created the Polo name to brand them. He sold them by visiting stores around New York, pulling up outside in a vintage Morgan sports car and wearing an old flying jacket. Shirts and suits quickly followed

and so were the beginnings of what would become a multi-billion-dollar global enterprise – by 1970 Lauren was named America's best menswear designer.

Lauren has said that his appreciation for clothing came from the fact that, following the American Dream, he is a self-made man, coming from very little: 'Sometimes, being born without money can be a blessing – I had to go out and earn the money to buy clothes and anything I bought was very precious to me. I think this made me sensitive to the value of things that last.'

BOB MARLEY

1945 – 1981

Bob Marley poses for a publicity shot.

Alongside Che Guevara – a man with whom he shared a love of combat jackets – Bob Marley's fashion presence might be regarded as the greatest of the twentieth century. After all, his image, like Guevara's, has graced the front of endless T-shirts. And well into the twenty-first century that image continued to be licensed out to countless clothing lines (even a cannabis brand), some launched by Marley's descendants, and even inspired fashion collections from the likes of Fendi and Dior. It is an irony perhaps for a man who once suggested that his life was, after being born into poverty, a search for an identity.

But the style of the Jamaican reggae star himself was considerably more nuanced than the T-shirt graphics might suggest – focused around ganja and the colours of Rastafarianism as they often are. Certainly, Marley was a promoter of the symbolism of those colours – gold for the wealth of Africa, green for its natural abundance, red for the blood of martyrs. And certainly his dreadlocks – typically also a focus for said graphics – were distinctive at a time when Rastafarianism, Marley's adopted religion, was little known about outside of its native Ethiopia. This in turn ensured that Marley was also identifiable by his preference for hats that could keep his dreads in order – beanies and slouch hats in particular.

But what most clearly expressed his personality was the essentially laid-back, basic and inexpensive approach he took to the way he dressed (the advice that 'money can't buy life' constituted his dying words at the age of just 36). Hard-wearing – and hard-worn – denim shirts, tracksuit jackets and army surplus garments were individualistic given his celebrity – the surplus perhaps also nodding to his self-described role as a 'revolutionary' – but also reflected both the clothes of the counterculture and, by turns, those of the worker. Of course, they also followed the diktats of his religion to dress simply and unostentatiously.

It was a distinct change from Marley's more performance-orientated style when, before his solo career, he played as part of the Wailers: Bunny Wailer's girlfriend of the time, Jean Watt, was a dressmaker and provided the band with fitted shirts in loud African prints; at the time Marley also wore his hair in an Afro. But, all the same, the more down-home style Marley later favoured was one he wore the rest of his life. It has often been described as effortless – most accurately because Marley, it seems, barely gave much thought to what he was wearing. He was more interested in being a key musical – even moral and religious – figure than making a style statement.

Bob Marley, ca.1980, pioneering a sportswear-heavy
look of green tracksuit top and purple sweatpants,
with his crocheted cap.

'MONEY CAN'T
BUY LIFE.'

Bob Marley performing at the Crystal Palace Bowl, London,
in 1980, his jacket made in the colours of the Ethiopian flag.

Marley revealing his fondness for
hard-wearing denims.

Marley in military surplus.

BOB MARLEY

MARCELLO MASTROIANNI

1924 – 1996

The closing shot of arguably Mastroianni's
most famous film, *La Dolce Vita*.

Marcello Mastroianni once half joked that his mentor, the film director Federico Fellini, had been planning a film with Paul Newman and was considering Mastroianni for a role because he needed someone 'ordinary looking', so as not to steal the star's limelight. In the end the legend of the golden age of Italian cinema stole the role – Newman had been the studio's choice for the lead in *La Dolce Vita*. 'My legs are skinny, my face has no power or resolve,' Mastroianni said. 'They [referring to Hollywood's leading men] knew where they were going – or, at least, we presumed they knew. I haven't any idea. If they were heroes, then I'm a non-hero.'

Except, perhaps, when it came to matters of style. If Mastroianni, a double Palme d'Or winner, was circumspect about his job – acting is, he said, to the *Washington Post*, 'a particularly fortunate profession. I am in perpetual infancy. It is like playing cops and robbers forever' – his impact on men's dress, especially in his native Italy, cannot have escaped him.

Not quite the suave Latin lover that his reputation and stereotype suggested, this nevertheless contributed to his being regarded as a benchmark of Italian post-war cool: stripped back, lean and monochromatic – certainly when compared with the baggier tailoring of America's Ivy League style of the time –

this was a sharp, slim, distinctly European suiting wrapped in a bohemian scarf and topped with impenetrable dark glasses and a cigarette as smouldering as the implied sexuality of the style. This was a twentieth-century embodiment of ideas close to the Italian psyche for centuries – of '*sprezzatura*', what sixteenth-century Italian writer Baldassare Castiglione posited as the 'universal rule in all human affairs', a facade of nonchalance that concealed the artistry required to pull off challenges with aplomb; and of '*la bella figura*', 'the beautiful figure', the need to maintain a permanent, impermeable shell of unruffled chic.

Costume designers such as Piero Gherardi knew how Mastroianni's wardrobe – closely inspected by audiences – could prove powerfully symbolic, its graphic rigour a counter to the character of ennui, frustration and puzzlement he often played. Certainly, while Hollywood actors routinely had their bodies eroticized on-screen by the 1950s and 1960s, against the norm Mastroianni typically remained very much dressed up. In *La Dolce Vita*, Mastroianni's character goes through a kind of conversion – he starts the film in black suits and white shirts, the fashion of the time, and ends up in white suits with black shirts, at odds with the urban environment that was his playground. When Mastroianni died in 1996, Rome dimmed

Mastroianni photographed
on a walk in Milan, 1971.

'THE DAY WHEN EVERYONE IS VERY, VERY ELEGANT, I WILL START TO GO AROUND DRESSED LIKE A TRAMP.'

Marcello Mastroianni in the garden of the Villa Foscari 'La Malcontenta'
during a break in shooting the film *Casanova 70*, in 1964.

Marcello Mastroianni, not such a rose between thorns, in summer suiting between actresses Jester Naefe and Isabelle Corey.

Marcello Mastroianni in pale double-breasted suit, in Venice in 1957.

the lights and shut off the water at the Trevi Fountain, a nod to the scene in the film in which he wades into it, fully suited, with Anita Ekberg.

But Mastroianni's influence was all the more sustained – in effect becoming the definition of Italian male dressing for decades to follow – because he dressed off-screen much as he did on-screen, with discretion and understatement. 'I hate fashion,' the actor once opined. 'Fashion and designer labels. ... It is so stupid for people to pay all these high prices just to have

the designer's name in a coat.' Habitually, he ordered 12 suits a year from Vittorio Zenobi, his tailor in Rome, favouring English cloths, and had his shoes made by Lobb. Dressing well mattered to him, chiefly as a point of pride and of distinction. 'The day when everyone is very, very elegant,' he told a reporter in 1964, 'I will start to go around dressed like a tramp.'

MARCELLO MASTROIANNI

STEVE MCQUEEN

1930 – 1980

Steve McQueen, easy in a Wrangler denim shirt, on the set of the film *Baby the Rain Must Fall*, 1965.

Don Gordon, Steve McQueen's co-star in *Bullitt*, aptly summed up McQueen's appeal. 'Like his character in [*The Great Escape*], he was cool, together, abstracted from the group, his own guy. Of course, he could also be a shit, too, but that was all part of the appeal.' A certain detachment, sometimes ironic, sometimes unreadable, has long been considered an essential ingredient of this nebulous quality we call cool, and McQueen – oft dubbed the 'King of Cool', not to mention the 'Cooler King', after his character in *The Great Escape* – had that to spare; indeed, his accepted cool would become a matter of cliché.

Small wonder that, over the years following his death in 1980, many companies in the fashion industry sought to make capital from his cool by creating 'Steve McQueen' lines specifically inspired by his connection with them, such as sunglasses manufacturer Persol – the actor often wore Persol 714 blue-tinted, tortoiseshell-framed sunglasses – or watchmaker TAG Heuer – McQueen wore one of its Monaco watches in *Le Mans*.

Many actors have come to be associated with a distinctly masculine stylishness – typically a product of the costume designer's efforts more than their own. McQueen certainly gained from assistance – Theodora Van Runkle and Ron Postal, who dressed him in Douglas Hayward suits for *The Thomas Crown Affair*, once recorded that they had to try on 30 pairs of trousers 'to get the right ones to make his behind look great' – but he also embodied that masculinity in his own right.

Indeed, his first wife, Neile Adams, encouraged McQueen to embody it, to make it a central tenet of his screen presence – it was she who suggested he wear sleeves only to the elbow so that his forearms became the focal point of his sex appeal; note how in *The Great Escape*, McQueen would spent much of his screen time in a blue sweatshirt with sleeves cut off at the elbow. He supplemented this with a personal wardrobe of sportswear and casual classics: Baracuta G9 Harrington jackets and slim cords; jeans and suede boots (so-called 'Playboy' boots by makers Hutton); polo necks and khakis; V- and polo-neck sweaters, shawl cardigans and tweed jackets. It was, as McQueen's son Chad would identify, 'his persona was about flying under the radar, being stylish but low-key'.

Clearly costume designers were often keen to retain that McQueen style when possible – anachronistically, in *The Cincinnati Kid* (1965) he wears a velvet-collared waxed jacket of the kind he favoured for motorcycle racing, despite the film being set during the Great Depression. Such was the style that saw him selected in the same year to be the first male cover of *Harper's Bazaar*.

Steve McQueen, in 1974, the year he starred with
fellow style icon Paul Newman in *The Towering Inferno*.

'I'D RATHER WAKE UP IN THE MIDDLE OF NOWHERE THAN IN ANY CITY ON EARTH.'

McQueen in *The Great Escape*, 1963, wearing khakis and sweatshirt with cut-off sleeves.

Bullitt, 1968, one of the seminal McQueen looks – black polo-neck sweater, brown tweed suit, brown suede boots.

Steve McQueen with his daughter Terry in Los
Angeles in 1964 – wearing the Baracuta Harrington
jacket that would become a favourite.

McQueen in *The Thomas Crown Affair*,
1968, as the dapper gentleman thief.

Not that McQueen only played at machismo: his wardrobe was underscored by action. He raced cars, flew planes and rode motorbikes as much for hobbies as he did in his films – stunts he often did himself; he was fiercely competitive – he insisted on exactly the same number of lines and equal billing to his co-star in *The Towering Inferno* Paul Newman; he was an outdoorsman – 'I'd rather wake up in the middle of nowhere than in any city on earth,' he once told *Life* magazine; and while he was keen to extend his range beyond 'those tough, uptight types', as McQueen called them – one reason why he played bespoke-suited, debonair and refined in *The Thomas Crown Affair* – he had a certain disdain for his art, giving it all up at the peak of his stardom, growing a beard and dropping out. His rebelliousness saw him widely disliked by directors – but loved as a hero figure.

JIM MORRISON

1943 – 1971

The earliest known studio portrait
of Jim Morrison, date unknown.

When The Doors played *The Ed Sullivan Show* in 1967, the producers asked them to change a lyric in 'Light My Fire' in objection to its reference to drugs. Jim Morrison, the band's charismatic front man, sang it his way anyhow. The band was promptly banned from the show. By then Morrison had already started to shape the contemporary perception of the rock star, in attitude and in attire.

As a student of photography and film – the artistic medium he expected to end up working in exclusively – he perhaps appreciated the importance of image more than many of his contemporaries. Teamed with the stance of a rock philosopher – 'I am interested in anything about revolt, disorder, chaos – especially activity that seems to have no meaning,' as Morrison put it, 'it seems to me to be the road toward freedom' – it was a potent blend. Here was someone ready to break the rules – he was arrested a number of times, including once for rioting and once for exposing himself on stage – and, seemingly, to live with few regrets. 'Some of the worst mistakes in my life

were haircuts,' as Morrison noted. He once described himself as 'ideally suited for the work I'm doing'.

The band's dark, psychedelic music needed a dark, poetic, mysterious leader and Morrison's devil-may-care approach was mirrored in his long, curly hair and bohemian, part-hippy, part-Hades dress, worn both on stage and off: loose, Byronic white or black linen shirts, silver concho belts and bead necklaces – a product of a fascination with Native American culture Morrison had had since he was four, when he witnessed a car crash involving Native Americans – Chelsea boots, fringed suede jackets, aviator sunglasses and black, shiny, skintight leather trousers. Morrison may not have been the first rock star to wear these – Gene Vincent might stake a claim here, one dating to the mid 1950s – but it was the overt sexuality he channelled through his that made leather trousers a rock staple.

Indeed, Morrison looked as though he lived in his – perhaps inspiring his long-term girlfriend, Pamela Courson, to run her own boutique in Los Angeles, specializing in more

Morrison, photographed in Los Angeles in 1967.

'I AM INTERESTED IN ANYTHING ABOUT REVOLT, DISORDER, CHAOS – ESPECIALLY ACTIVITY THAT SEEMS TO HAVE NO MEANING.'

Morrison on stage in tight denims.

The Doors posing in Germany in 1968.
Left to right: Ray Manzarek, Jim Morrison,
Robby Krieger and John Densmore.

sophisticated takes on the fashion of the US counterculture. Certainly Morrison only later in life abandoned the look in favour of jeans and T-shirts when a portliness began to overtake the svelte sexiness of the self-proclaimed 'Lizard King', for which he had become internationally idolized. By then, his dress had defined many of the tropes of the rock-star uniform, with the likes of Iggy and the Stooges' Iggy Pop, Velvet Revolver's Scott Weiland and The Strokes' Julian Casablancas acknowledging their style debt to Morrison.

'Here's this guy, out of his head on acid, dressed in leather with his hair all oiled and curled,' recalled Iggy Pop, speaking to writer Jeb Wright of the first time he saw Jim Morrison. 'It got confrontational. ... He's really pissing people off and he's lurching around making these guys angry. ... [And] it was sort of a case of, "Hey, I can do that."'

Morrison on stage during a 1968 concert at the Hollywood Bowl.

JIM MORRISON

PAUL NEWMAN

1925 – 2008

Paul Newman, black tie and
beard, at the International Film
Festival, Venice, 1962.

Beyond his film roles, Paul Newman was the epitome of preppy: button-down shirts, V-neck sweaters, shawl-collared cardigans, slim khakis, blazers and a personal favourite of his, Keds or Sperry Striper canvas sneakers and, of course, the Rolex Daytona Cosmograph watch that was named after him. One of the most captivating shots of him as a young man, by Eve Arnold, is an apt summary: white T-shirt, with turn-ups, loose trousers, white socks, loafers.

Indeed, while Newman was used to wearing a tuxedo – he was nominated for nine Academy Awards, winning one for *The Color of Money* – the actor, philanthropist and record-breaking racing-car driver was more used to masculine, outdoorsy, workmanlike clothing, the kind of clothes in which he would pass much of his free time fishing the Islamorada, Florida. Small wonder, perhaps, when he grew up working as a clerk in his father's sporting goods store, or even that on graduation from college he launched a student-run laundry business.

He favoured the ordinary clothes of an ordinary man – which he insisted he was, noting that he didn't think he had any natural gift to be anything. 'I don't think Paul Newman really thinks he is Paul Newman,' as the screenwriter William

Goldman had it. 'It's only when you're away from California that you cannot take yourself seriously,' said Newman, referring to his decision to live in a remote, rural setting in Westport, Connecticut. Certainly he is said to have never felt quite at home in black tie – style lore has it that he burned all of his dinner suits on a bonfire on his seventy-fifth birthday.

Newman's was a ruggedness that was captured in many of the nonconformist, sometimes cocky, sometimes caddish parts he often played – whether, to cite just two examples, the sun-faded work shirt and chore jackets of *Cool Hand Luke* or the Levi's and western clothing of *Hud*, the film that made him a superstar. Such parts – and the method-acting style behind them – saw him and his fellow generation of actors represent a new mode in masculinity: self-doubting, cynical, more men of internal lives than men of action.

But it was a ruggedness countered by the fact that he was – with his Greek-statuary bone structure and ice-blue eyes – widely considered handsome beyond compare to all but a few, and retained his looks well into middle age. 'There's something very corrupting about being an actor,' he told the *New York Times*. 'It places a terrible premium on appearance.'

Paul Newman on the set of the comedy western *Pocket Money* in Tucsan, Arizona, 1972.

Paul Newman cradles a soda bottle under one arm while digging into a bag
of snacks in front of a stall selling Mexican souvenirs, California, 1955.

Newman leans against a fence, smoking a cigarette, on the set of the film *Hud*, Texas, 1962

Paul Newman in 1955.

'TO WORK AS HARD AS I'VE WORKED TO ACCOMPLISH ANYTHING AND THEN HAVE SOME YO-YO COME UP AND SAY, "TAKE OFF THOSE DARK GLASSES AND LET'S HAVE A LOOK AT THOSE BLUE EYES," IS REALLY DISCOURAGING.'

His fame – at odds with his being a largely private man – led him to often wear disguises in public, putting on beards and dark glasses. Fans would ask him to remove the latter. Newman would tell them if he took off his glasses, his pants would fall down. On other occasions he was more direct: 'To work as hard as I've worked to accomplish anything and then have some yo-yo come up and say, "Take off those dark glasses and let's have a look at those blue eyes," is really discouraging.'

PAUL NEWMAN

TOMMY NUTTER

1943 – 1992

Tommy Nutter in his shop in 1969 – wearing the
wide-lapelled, flared-trouser style that would
define the following decade for men.

Tommy Nutter dressed the part. Aptly named as far as his Savile Row peers might have considered it, Nutter was trained as a traditional bespoke tailor with Donaldson, Williams & Ward – albeit only once he'd given up a planned career in plumbing – after his interest was sparked through buying his first bespoke suit from Burton, aged fifteen. But Nutter quickly grew tired of the traditionalism that Savile Row – the spiritual home of tailoring – then embodied. After all, this was 1968 – London was 'swinging', and the Establishment was being rocked in many ways.

Nutter, with his bouffant hair and distinctive, avant-garde suits – with a modern if slightly period flair, all wide shoulders and peak lapels, narrow waists, long jackets, parallel-legged trousers and strong pattern – stood apart, as much a stylist as a tailor. Tweed checks, and clashing checks, and outlandishly wide 'Oxford bag' trousers became signatures.

Indeed, he dressed more like the rock royalty who also wore his suits. As Elton John, one of his customers, once noted: Nutter 'completely glamorized Savile Row and made it accessible'. Mick Jagger became a customer, as did Eric Clapton, The Rolling Stones' Charlie Watts, Vidal Sassoon and David Hockney. The Beatles (excluding a denim-clad George Harrison) wore Nutter designs for the cover of their *Abbey Road* album. But then Nutter was in part financially backed by Peter Brown, Managing Director of The Beatles' Apple Corps, as well as British singer Cilla Black. Ringo Starr starred in advertisements for the tailor, contrary to band policy opposing such endorsements.

Nutter – both in the much-copied way he dressed himself, and in the way he presented the idea of bespoke tailoring to a clientele previously alien to it – changed the face of Savile Row, much as Hardy Amies had done for a generation before. He made what until then had been a dusty Establishment world largely closed to all but dusty Establishment types a place of interest to his contemporaries – albeit somewhat by accident, simply by doing what seemed natural to the times. That meant not only moving on tailoring but also the way it was presented. In 1969, he and his business partner, tailor Edward Sexton, opened premises with shop windows – commonplace to other menswear shops but then unheard of on Savile Row.

Tommy Nutter in Edwardian style
meets the 1970s, in New York.

Nutter in 1973 wearing an outfit of his own design –
bringing together checks of many sizes and colours.

Nutter in 1973 with singer Cilla Black, herself wearing a white trouser suit designed by him. Black was an early investor in his business.

Tommy Nutter wearing a single-breasted blazer in royal-blue flannel, dove-grey tattersall check wrap-over waistcoat, pink block-striped shirt with white collar and cuffs and deeply pleated trousers, in the late 1980s.

Admittedly, Nutter's window displays – one featured patchouli-soaked stuffed rats wearing diamond chokers – were less commonplace.

'We didn't know what we would do would create a furore,' as Sexton has said. 'We were just two young guys who liked looking in shop windows, so we thought nothing of putting in shop windows. We didn't know that challenged tradition. But that then allowed new ideas about tailoring to spread through a very closed world. Even the timing was right – London then encouraged a cult of innovation. It was luck. I've been extremely lucky in life – none of it was planned.'

Nutter's time centre-stage was brief – Sexton bought him out of the business just seven years after it opened, but continued to cut suits under the Nutter name until 1983. Nutter himself went to work for another Savile Row tailor, during which time he designed Jack Nicholson's costume for his role as the Joker in *Batman*.

PABLO PICASSO

1881 – 1973

Pablo Picasso in 1935 – although typically photographed in relaxed style, the artist also had a penchant for British tailoring.

Few men come to be known for a single garment but those who do perhaps share an understanding of the symbolic impact of attachment to a style with which they can be readily associated – it becomes a kind of calling card. This is maybe why it is so true of politicians in particular – Anthony Eden and his homburg, Jawaharlal Nehru's collarless jackets, Mao Zedong's Zhongshan tunic, Kim Jong Il's safari suits.

But an artist might well also appreciate this too – Pablo Picasso certainly did, given the strong connection in the mind's eye between the Spaniard and that most iconic of Basque/French clothing, the striped Breton top. Its graphic simplicity – traditionally 21 navy hoops on a white background; its man-of-the-people roots – it was worn by fishermen and sailors before it found any place in fashion; its later hint of a wealthy, bohemian, Mediterranean lifestyle – all played to shape Picasso's public image beyond, of course, the revolutionary nature of his art. The Breton was his personal take on the artist's smock – he favoured

a style that left the neckline and upper arms free of stripes.

Picasso had, however, enjoyed a lifelong love of clothes, and especially English clothes. He first visited England in 1919 to design scenery and costumes for a Ballets Russes production of *The Three-Cornered Hat* – the result was a mix of Victorian flounces and, perhaps prefiguring his regard for the Breton, vertical stripes. But he had long harboured a high regard for English style. Once in London, and having requested that art critic and curator Clive Bell be his guide, Picasso spent much of the time on shopping trips to Savile Row and the East End to buy three-piece suits, as well as other paraphernalia of quintessentially English dress at the time, such as watch chains and bowler hats. Picasso's father, José Ruiz Blasco, also an artist, no doubt proved some inspiration for this fascination – such was his love of English style that he was nicknamed 'El Inglés'.

But it was a more casual summertime style with which Picasso would come to be connected: photographer Arnold

A photograph of Picasso taken by Robert
Doisneau in 1952 at Vallauris, France.

Picasso at his home in Cannes, 1960,
showing an artist's eye for mixing bold
stripes with muted checks.

Pablo Picasso, in 1935, wearing a double-breasted grey flannel
suit. He's standing in front of a 1917 portrait of his wife Olga.

Newman's portrait of Picasso in his studio in Cannes in 1956
shows him in a thick, burgundy terry cloth polo shirt, as if he
had come fresh from a swim. He might typically wear espadrilles
too – another homespun style of Spanish origin, which further
underscored his relaxed dress, a uniform that allowed him to
focus on his art. By this time, Picasso's graphic style was finding
expression in aspects of fashion itself, specifically in jewellery
design. Among his pieces were small 'bull' pendants in silver or
gold. Atypically, of course, Picasso had them cast by his dentist.

'I'D LIKE TO LIVE AS A POOR MAN WITH LOTS OF MONEY.'

Picasso smoking a cigarette, in Cannes, France,
in 1956 – he wears a favourite towelling top.

PABLO PICASSO

ELVIS PRESLEY

1935 – 1977

Elvis in Las Vegas, 1956, wearing a
loose-fit jacket over a bare chest.

Such was the visual impact of many of Elvis Presley's Las Vegas stage costumes, notably those of the 1970s – the Bill Belew-designed, high-collared, gemstone-encrusted white jumpsuits, the skintight, top-to-toe black leather, the outlandish sunglasses – that his stylishness as a private individual was typically overlooked. 'In public, I like real conservative clothes, something that's not too flashy,' Presley once noted. 'But on stage I like them as flashy as you can get them.'

That influence might well have been inevitable – he was, after all, one of the most important cultural figures of the twentieth century, having had the most top-40 hits, the most top-10 hits, the most weeks at number one in the charts and sales of over one billion records, as well as, critically for his role as a style leader, being the first rock star to cross over to commercially successful films.

But that influence was also deserved: away from the eye-popping performance garb, Presley's blend of rockabilly and Southern Christian boy saw him still keen to be bold in his presentation. Details mattered – he liked his custom-made gold jewellery, most famously his diamond 'Taking Care of Business' initial ring; and, inspired by his time as a truck driver (it was

the style worn by truckers of the 1950s) wore his signature, dyed-black hair in a longer, pompadour style, later maintained by Larry Geller, founder of Hollywood's first men-only salon turned Presley's personal hair stylist.

He favoured his bespoke shirts, with elastic added at cuff and elbow to give the sleeves volume, and suits by Sy Devore – Frank Sinatra's tailor – but also was loyal to outfitters Lansky Bros. on Beale Street, Memphis, where he had shopped as a young man. Proprietor Bernard Lansky fitted him out in pegged pants and two-tone shoes, dressed him for his early TV appearances, on the likes of *The Ed Sullivan Show* and Jimmy and Tommy Dorsey's *Stage Show*, and chose the white suit and blue tie that Presley was buried in. 'I put his first suit on him and his last suit on him,' as Lanksy had it.

Distinctively, Presley was also ready to wear strong colours, this, of course, from the man who had sung about protecting his 'Blue Suede Shoes'. Few men would wear clashing prints as he did, but fewer still would wear bubblegum pink, his favourite colour, until Presley made it acceptable – pink shirts, belts, socks were all part of his wardrobe. But then the more obviously macho black leather also figured, even if denim did

Presley's open-collar, loose-fit jacket style allowed him to move – and move millions of
young women in the process. Here he performs on *The Milton Berle Show*, 1956.

Presley in the 1950s.

Elvis Presley making his first appearance
on *The Ed Sullivan Show* – from the waist
up at least – in Los Angeles, 1956.

Presley in the classic gold lamé suit, tailored by Nudie's Rodeo
Tailors in North Hollywood, and ordered at a cost of $2,500 by
Colonel Parker. Presley wore it only four times.

Elvis Presley on tour in 1972, wearing one of the rhinestone jumpsuit
costumes – designed by Manuel Martinez, then of Nudie's Rodeo
Tailors – that would define the Elvis stereotype.

Presley hadn't performed for seven years by the time of his 'Elvis '68 Comeback Special'. The leather jacket and trousers echoed those of Jim Morrison.

'IN PUBLIC, I LIKE REAL CONSERVATIVE CLOTHES, SOMETHING THAT'S NOT TOO FLASHY ... BUT ON STAGE I LIKE THEM AS FLASHY AS YOU CAN GET THEM.'

Elvis Presley thinks about purchasing a shirt at Supreme Men's Shop (on Broadway), New York, 1956.

not: Presley associated jeans with the poverty of his childhood, and normally refused to wear them as a grown man unless a film role demanded it.

His awareness of his style extended – as it did for many in the public eye to this level of intensity – to vanity: in 1973, he had a hair transplant and his teeth capped (he inhaled one loose cap during a rehearsal and spent several days in hospital as a consequence). But this never overshadowed the fact that Presley's style had, by then, done much to redefine masculine dress – not as conservative as Presley may have thought he wore, but as colourful, expressive, even entertaining. Few others would turn up to meet the President of the United States in white shirt with exaggerated collar, a gold-buttoned black coat and a belt with a huge buckle, as Presley did to meet Nixon in 1970. And he looked good in it too.

ROBERT REDFORD

b. 1936

Robert Redford in 1975.

It is only occasionally that a character's costume and a personal style coincide. But it happened for Robert Redford, as Joseph Turner, the CIA researcher on the run in *Three Days of the Condor*. Indeed, in one interview, the director was taken aback to be asked about Redford's clothing. 'He wore one outfit through the whole picture!' Sydney Pollack exclaimed.

But that outfit – hiking boots, dark sweater over pale-blue cowboy shirt, loose tie, faded jeans and single-breasted, grey herringbone tweed jacket – saw the film cited as one of the most stylish of all time. The look is professorial, easy, prefiguring a style taken global by Ralph Lauren, accented by key details – the gold-rimmed aviator glasses, the DOXA Sharkhunter watch. If the character had driven a car, it might have been something vintage – a 1955 Porsche 550 RS Spyder, Redford's own choice. The actor long favoured a classic Rolex Submariner too.

His wardrobe in *Three Days of the Condor* was a conservative, western-inspired look that, with a knitted tie and other variations, Redford not only revisited in other films – such as *All The President's Men* – but made his own for life, adding in dark-rimmed glasses and leather bomber jackets. It suited a great-outdoors life away from Hollywood (with his first paycheque Redford started to buy up land in Utah, and by 1975 had acquired 7,000 acres (2,833 hectares), including mountains,

a ranch, a horse-training farm) but also informed the casual, bohemian, WASPish uniform of Sundance, the independent film-makers' festival and enclave he founded in 1980. Indeed, Sundance even operated a catalogue business, chock-full of products – plaid shirts, chunky cardigans – that represented the 'Sundance lifestyle'.

It was a look that ran counter to the period style with which Redford came to be associated through many of his biggest films: *The Way We Were*, set in the 1930s to 1950s, *Butch Cassidy and the Sundance Kid* and, most strikingly, *The Great Gatsby*, with costume design by Ralph Lauren – although Redford was subsequently seen pulling off his own combination of wide-pinstriped double-breasted suit, chambray shirt and baker's boy plaid cap.

But certainly Redford's general consistency in his all-American style – and his defining mop of unruly hair – gave him a distinction that some thought, all acting talent aside, he would never achieve. *Butch Cassidy and the Sundance Kid* screenwriter William Goldman once recalled a studio executive dismissing Redford: 'He's just another Californian blonde. Throw a stick out of a window in Malibu, you'll hit six like him.' How wrong he proved to be.

Redford wearing a cowboy hat and sunglasses
in *Little Fauss and Big Halsy*, 1970.

Robert Redford in western style on a cliff along
the Green River in Browns Park, Utah.

Redford in *The Candidate*, 1972.

'WHEN I WAS A KID, NOBODY
TOLD ME I WAS GOOD-LOOKING.
I WISH THEY HAD. I WOULD'VE
HAD A BETTER TIME.'

Redford in perhaps his most stylish movie, *Three Days of the Condor*, 1975.

Redford in costume for a publicity portrait used to promote *Butch Cassidy and the Sundance Kid*, 1969.

ROBERT REDFORD

KEITH RICHARDS

b. 1943

Keith Richards in Los Angeles in 1988.

When once asked to name his personal style icon Keith Richards responded, 'Why should I? I am one.' It's a rock 'n' roll statement from one of rock 'n' roll's most distinctive dressers – be that his blend of trench coat, silk shirts and skinny jeans, fedora or trademark bandana (and sometimes both at the same time), framing kohled eyes, and wrapped around the hair he has cut himself since first pocketing the money his mother gave him every two weeks to go to the barber's.

Then there is the excess jewellery (or 'my silver' as Richards calls it): his Courts and Hackett skull ring – supposedly a reminder that beauty is only skin deep – and his handcuff bracelet – supposedly a reminder never to get arrested again. Both pieces have been worn consistently since the late 1970s, often together with a mess of necklaces and piratical hoop earrings, all conspiring to make him the inspiration for Johnny Depp's portrayal of Captain Jack Sparrow in *Pirates of the Caribbean*. Indeed, with a flamboyance that Richards' fellow band member Mick Jagger has retained mostly

for performances, Richards has lived his bohemian, anti-Establishment look from his first days in the band, whether on stage or not. 'Just be yourself is all I can say – the rest of it's a fucking joke,' he told *NME*.

Yet despite wearing what might seem a disparate collection of found garments – one 1970s photo has him in leopard-skin coat, Breton top, Japanese-print scarf and outsized, polka-dot bow tie – the guitarist made their assembled, avant-garde effect uniquely his own and, just as important, stuck with the formula. 'Some things get better with age. Like me,' suggested the man who often borrowed clothes from his then-girlfriend Anita Pallenberg and later his wife Patti Hansen. Certainly Louis Vuitton thought he embodied a distinctive style of his own making, signing him to front an ad campaign in 2008.

'There was some page in *Vogue* and I was a fashion icon. Charlie [Watts], who spends half his time on Savile Row, said [disparagingly of Richards], "You, a fashion icon?!",' Richards once reported to *GQ*. 'I'm the kind of guy who when I wake up

Keith Richards in 1972.

Keith Richards of The Rolling Stones poses during the filming of the video for 'Waiting on a Friend' in New York, 1981.

'YOU'VE GOT THE SUN, YOU'VE GOT THE MOON, AND YOU'VE GOT THE ROLLING STONES.'

Richards playing in London in 2013 – his rock 'n' roll style in older age tempered to bandana, jewellery and scarves.

Keith Richards and Brian Jones in Hyde Park, 1967 – dressed more in the Carnaby Street style of London's 'Swinging Sixties'.

Richards in 1974 – cigarette, guitar, stripes, spots,
animal print, effortlessly all at once.

I'm not aware of anything for half an hour. I pick up whatever's around and put it on. I don't think about it. I said to Charlie, "Look at that picture in *Vogue* and you'll see the buttons are on the wrong side of the shirt. All I did was put on Anita's clothes …".'

Watts, in fact, was more complimentary of his less traditionally dapper band mate's style: 'The way Keith dresses is amazing,' he said in 1979. 'Often I'll put on one of his belts or something made of tapestry and it looks ridiculous on me. Keith has beautiful style. He has a way of putting on clothes that I'd never dream of.'

KEITH RICHARDS

FRANK SINATRA

1915 – 1998

Frank Sinatra, posed for a publicity shot
in the 1940s, wearing a windowpane
check suit, his tie artfully undone and
tucked into his waistband.

Frank Sinatra loved hats. Part security blanket, part attitude, Sinatra's hat didn't even come off while he recorded. His most legendary records, made with Capitol during the 1950s, were when the most indelible images of 'Ol' Blue Eyes' were formed. 'As Sinatra stands up to the mike, tie loose and blue palmetto hat stuck on awry, his cigarette hung slackly from his lips, a mood curls out into the room like smoke,' *Time* magazine noted of one session. As Stan Cornyn, the liner-note writer for several Sinatra albums pointed out, in a hat Sinatra looked 'what your mother used to call "natty". His wide-banded hat is tipped back, one inch off straight flat.' 'Angles are attitudes,' as Sinatra once opined, of the crucial way a hat should be worn.

Sinatra was said to have some 20 hats during those years, all made exclusively for him by Cavanagh, but it was the snap-brim with which he would come to be associated – the hat he might push on to the heads of his pals during late-night carousing, denoting that it was their turn to sing. Ironically, perhaps, he took up wearing a hat only as a way of dealing with his receding hairline in public. 'He didn't realize what a tumult

it would start,' his daughter Nancy noted. To a generation, Sinatra's hat became symbolic of what it was to be debonair.

But Sinatra was more than his hat. As a child in Hoboken he was known, derisively, as 'Slacksey O'Brien' for his fancy trousers. He had 13 sports jackets by the time he reached high school. His job as a copy boy at the local newspaper brought him money inevitably to spend on yet more. By the 1960s he had some 150 suits. His wardrobe was said to have regimental order. 'I am a symmetrical man, almost to a fault,' he once noted of himself in a piece published by *Life* magazine. 'I demand everything in its place. My clothing must hang just so.'

Yet Sinatra was no square. Lavender – Agua Lavanda Puig in particular – was not just a favourite fragrance for this overly hygienic man (he might shower and change three times a day), it was a favourite colour for his clothing; pink as well. Far from adhering to any notion of his times that it might be unmanly to wear colour, Sinatra embraced it. 'Orange is the happiest colour,' he said, a notion he took to heart, from his Oxford-cloth shirts to his swimming trunks to the pocket handkerchiefs he wore

More Frank than ever – Sinatra in 1958 at the height of his star power.

Sinatra takes some tourist snaps in Berlin, 1960.

Above left, Sinatra in 1954 – the loosened
tie would become one of his sartorial motifs
– and earlier in 1950, above right.

with his tuxedo. His golf clothing gave him more opportunity to really embrace this idea, with his 'alpacas' – baggy-sleeved, loose-fitting cardigans that he bought by the dozen – racking up a $30,000-a-year knitwear bill at the Palm Springs Canyon Club store.

Certainly Sinatra had his sartorial rules and sensitivities. Details mattered. He habitually polished his shoes on the underside of couch cushions before every performance, something he did as a kid, winning his mother's reproach in the process. He wore his suits, by Sy Devore and later Carroll & Co., with three-button-cuffed shirts that buttoned beneath the crotch. His ties, typically by Sulka or Turnbull & Asser, had to be conservative, understated. 'I've never known a woman who could select neckties I really like,' Sinatra said. 'I think any gal who could do that ... would pass the supreme test.' And he eschewed jewellery, aside from cufflinks – typically bought from a Florida hustler called Swifty Morgan, who, with his wares, was granted access to Sinatra wherever he was working – and a pinkie ring with the family crest. He once had matching pinkie

rings made for himself and Dean Martin – Martin always wore his; Sinatra never did.

Indeed, he felt most at home and was most iconic in the dark shades and rigour of the tailoring in which he dressed to perform. That was what was proper. The colour brown offended Sinatra, especially after dark when, he said, only black or, at a push, midnight blue or charcoal were appropriate. He made his point by stuffing firecrackers into the shoes of any friends with the temerity to wear the shade. And Sinatra was outspoken when his rules were broken. On finding that *The Tonight Show* host Joey Bishop and other fellow guests were dressed in pale grey on one occasion, he did not hold back. 'This is a midnight show! You only go out in daytime with these grey suits,' Sinatra offered. After all, to him a tuxedo was, as he put it, 'a way of life'.

FRANK SINATRA

Sinatra, suited and in his high-crowned
fedora, at London Airport in 1961.

Sinatra during a recording session in a studio at
Capitol Records, early 1950s – even at work behind
the scenes he looked the part.

'COCK YOUR HAT –
ANGLES ARE ATTITUDES.'

Sinatra, Sammy Davis Jr, Dean Martin and an unidentified man during
a recording session for the film *Come Blow Your Horn*, ca.1963.

FRANK SINATRA

MARK TWAIN

1835 – 1910

A portrait of Mark Twain in
his signature white suit.

Mark Twain may be a literary giant but he had a passing interest as a fashion correspondent too. Writing for a US state newspaper, he would, for example, pass comment – often more in satire than seriousness – on the latest women's styles. 'I once made up my mind to keep the ladies of the State of Nevada posted upon the fashions, but I found it hard to do,' he wrote in 'The Fashions'. 'The fashions got so shaky that it was hard to tell what was good orthodox fashion, and what heretical and vulgar. This shakiness still obtains in everything pertaining to a lady's dress except her bonnet and her shoes.'

He would then advise a furtive glance under the hoops then worn to give a fullness to a lady's dress. 'It reminds me of how I used to peep under circus tents when I was a boy and see a lot of mysterious legs tripping about with no visible bodies attached to them,' he adds. 'And what handsome vari-colored, gold-clasped garters they wear nowadays!'

But the author of the *Adventures of Huckleberry Finn*, whose real name was Samuel Clemens, also had a more serious interest in clothing. In 1871, he had been issued one of the first US patents for what were described as 'Adjustable and Detachable Straps for Garments' that attached to everything from underpants to women's corsets and were designed as an alternative to suspenders, which Clemens was said to find uncomfortable.

Indeed, he would always go his own way in matters of dress, speaking out, in good humour, against fashions he disliked: '[Twenty-five years ago] no man was considered fully dressed until he donned a plug hat. Nowadays I think that no man is dressed until he leaves it home.' He had a sizeable moustache and wore his hair, with some notoriety, in an increasingly wild style that proclaimed his creative outsider nature. The *New York Times*' obituary even noted: 'It is a legend that he was vastly proud of his famous mop of white hair and used to spend the pains of a court lady in getting it to just the proper stage of artistic disarray.'

When Clemens received an honorary degree from Oxford University in 1907, he was so taken by the ceremonial gown he was given that he took to wearing it on other special occasions

Mark Twain photographed in
Hartford, Connecticut, ca.1905.

Mark Twain sitting outside in a wicker chair, wearing a
three-piece suit, bow tie and white straw hat, 1900.

'CLOTHES MAKE THE MAN – NAKED PEOPLE HAVE LITTLE OR NO INFLUENCE ON SOCIETY.'

too, including to his daughter's wedding. He advocated dress reform, notably the freedom for men to adopt elements of women's wardrobe ('goodness knows, they adopt enough of ours') – though his example of a cooling peek-a-boo waist was no doubt tongue in cheek.

But perhaps his greatest contribution to menswear – aside from the many bon mots he produced on the subject, most famously the notion that 'clothes make the man – naked people have little or no influence on society' – was his adoption of the white suit, prefiguring perhaps the style of late twentieth-century literary heavyweight Tom Wolfe.

Clemens first wore one to a congressional hearing in December 1906, so breaking with convention that newspaper reports of the important issue at hand were overshadowed by commentary on his bold and unseasonable choice of dress, until then associated with plantation owners and the suffocating summer heat of the Deep South. He is said to have had 14 white suits – one for each day, plus a daily change, so that he was never seen in a suit that appeared dirty.

Clemens subsequently played fast and loose with the truth of his reasons for taking up white flannel so enthusiastically, on one occasion simply saying that, having reached the age of 71, he had grown somewhat tired of the grey and drear men's attire he saw around him every day. 'The continual sight of drab clothing is likely to have a depressing effect,' he commented, adding, '… light-coloured clothing is more pleasing to the eye and enlivens the spirit. Now, of course, I cannot compel everyone to wear such clothing just for my especial benefit, so I do the next best thing and wear it myself.'

But maybe he hinted at another explanation in *Huckleberry Finn*. In that classic novel, one of his characters takes a more deliberately offensive regard to the power of the white suit to get one noticed. He determines, simply, to 'every day of his life … put on a clean shirt and a full suit from head to toe made out of linen so white it hurt your eyes to look at it'.

Twain, again in a white suit, in 1905 – he
preferred the lighter shade because,
he claimed, more sober clothes had a
negative effect on his spirits.

Twain, teaming a bowler hat with an
astrakhan-trimmed coat, in 1900.

MARK TWAIN

ANDY WARHOL

1928 – 1987

Andy Warhol in 1975 wearing
a preppy shirt and rep tie.

As pop artists took their inspiration from the imagery of the commercial world, it is perhaps no surprise that their work also fed into it. In 1962, Andy Warhol became one of the first to turn his work into fashion items when he began printing his *Campbell's Soup Cans* on to paper dresses, albeit as one-off garments for New York society women. Such was Warhol's stardom in the art world that three years later the Campbell Soup Company made what it called its 'Souper Dress', selling them for a dollar and a couple of labels from its cans. Pop art began to appear on designs from influential 1970s fashion houses, such as Biba and Mr Freedom, and on clothes seen on the backs of celebrities, such as Mick Jagger.

Yet Warhol's interest in fashion ran deep and not just because of his professional background as a window dresser and later an advertising illustrator for fashion magazines and stores Neiman Marcus and Barneys. Indeed, Warhol found department stores fascinating (they are 'kind of like museums', he once said). The crowd he ran with typically included figures influential in New York fashion circles, such as Roy Halston and Lee Radziwill, while Yves Saint Laurent and other fashion luminaries sat for their portrait. The Factory – Warhol's art-cum-social hub – was home to some of the most influential style-setters of 1960s New York. He also created *Interview*, his own fashion magazine. Indeed, his influence on fashion was arguably more in the milieu he fostered rather than the clothes he wore himself.

That said, he was conscious of his public image as an artist – perhaps even a new kind of artist, a brand. Warhol was also a keen experimenter in dress: bucking convention, he might wear paint-splattered trousers, a battered tuxedo jacket and yellow sunglasses to a black-tie event; or a dark jacket and tie with jeans. 'Fashion wasn't what you wore someplace anymore,' Warhol noted. 'It was the whole reason for going.' Having started to go bald in the 1950s, Warhol wore wigs – by turns yellow blonde, platinum blonde and then silvery grey – which became something of a signature. He had at least 40, made in New York by Paul Bochicchio using hair imported from Italy, and was clearly very attached to the persona they helped create. When a woman snatched his wig from his head at a book signing, he wrote later in his diary, 'I don't know what held me back from pushing her over the balcony.'

Certainly this self-described 'deeply superficial person'

Andy Warhol wearing a biker jacket over
a tailored one, in New York, 1968.

Andy Warhol at his New York house, by a photo of Shirley Temple, in 1966.

Andy Warhol in front of one of his pictures, in 1971.

Andy Warhol, preppy in seersucker, with the bleach blonde hair he would later cover with a variety of wigs.

Warhol in one of his trademark wigs,
wearing a tuxedo jacket casually.

'FASHION WASN'T WHAT YOU WORE SOMEPLACE ANYMORE; IT WAS THE WHOLE REASON FOR GOING.'

wore these symbols of his otherness, of his playing with the idea of identity, with no pretence at passing them off as his own hair – wild, often askew, with his own, darker hair poking out from underneath. He once framed one and gave it, as an artwork, to his friend and fellow distinctive dresser Jean-Michel Basquiat ('He was shocked,' Warhol noted). On other occasions he would wear theatrical masks, it is said to hide his skin problems; Warhol was intensely concerned with what he regarded as his physical flaws.

And yet, despite such flourishes, in many respects Warhol's dress was deeply conservative. While he liked a horizontally striped shirt or black polo-neck sweater and a pair of black Levi's 501 jeans, he was a lifelong fan of the American traditional preppiness of Brooks Brothers, whose neat suits,

button-down-collar shirts and penny loafers defined most of his wardrobe. Naturally, though, such clothes were worn with an element of subversion, with an irreverent schoolboy scruffiness that ensured his repp tie was rarely straight, his jacket and shirts were past their best and his shoes were typically unpolished, and sometimes not even laced up.

In effect, he made the uniform his own but embraced a uniform all the same. And with enthusiasm: the clothes he worked in he dubbed his 'paint clothes'. 'They're the same kind of clothes I wear every day, with paint on them,' he explained to Glen O'Brien of *Interview*. 'I have paint shoes and paint shirts and paint jackets and paint ties … And paint hankies.'

ORSON WELLES

1915 – 1985

Orson Welles, the boy genius, arriving
for the RKO Pictures Convention,
New York, 1940.

Looking chubby at the best of times, and positively portly later in life, Orson Welles' was perhaps an unlikely body on which to hang clothes stylishly. Yet the precocious renegade in art – genre busting in his radio productions and in his films (*Citizen Kane* most famously, of course) – was as much a renegade in the way he dressed.

Perhaps the inspiration came from the same source: a vision that knew it didn't fit in with conventional thinking, so didn't bother to try. 'Style,' as Welles put it, 'is knowing who you are, what you want to say, and not giving a damn.' And that from a man who, despite being in his prime years (his groundbreaking career highs were all during his twenties, and he featured on the cover of *Time* magazine at 23), was so self-conscious about his appearance, his nose especially, that he often took to wearing a prosthetic one for performances when the role didn't require it.

Perhaps, alternatively, it came from a healthy ego, as might develop when you are known as 'The Boy Wonder' to your circle. 'Good evening,' Welles is said to have introduced himself to a disappointingly sparsely populated theatre audience. 'I am Orson Welles – director, producer, actor, impresario, writer,

artist, magician, star of stage, screen and radio, and a pretty fair singer. Why are there so many of me and so few of you?'

Although often found in a suit – indeed, he designed many of his own suits, and dressing gowns, and had them made up by a tailor – Welles did it his own way, even when, later in life, his obesity reduced his suits to, as one friend called them 'a bifurcated tent' with all the lapels and pocket flaps attached to give the impression of a conventional suit. Welles is often credited, for example, with being the first to wear a suit with a T-shirt, rather than the shirt that the standards of the day required. Dressed more casually – on holiday with his then-wife Rita Hayworth – he would happily mix horizontal and vertical nautical stripes, again somewhat against the supposed rules of dress. He often sported a broad-brimmed hat and large scarf to suitably theatrical effect. His love of bow ties only grew as he got older – as did the size and flamboyance of the tie. And, at a time when others went clean cut, he sported a sizeable beard.

In dressing and looking the way he did, he rewrote notions of what a Hollywood star was meant to be – and all the more so because, while he could dress for the camera, he was never precious about his clothing. In 1947, while Welles was in Rome

Orson Welles in a studio portrait from the 1940s
– wearing a tailored jacket over a T-shirt, a look
he could claim to have pioneered.

Orson Welles – comfortably mixing different weights and directions of stripe – with wife Rita Hayworth on the beach in Miami, during the 1940s.

'STYLE IS KNOWING WHO YOU ARE, WHAT YOU WANT TO SAY, AND NOT GIVING A DAMN.'

Orson Welles, ca.1950.

Orson Welles – a larger man later in life who grew to favour a cape – potters with a golf club on his roof garden in 1967.

Welles was rarely at rest – when he was, he was found in a dressing gown, here in 1941.

to promote forthcoming film work, he wore a grey suit jacket and shirt with cufflinks, yet his clothes were described by one reporter as being adequate 'for an American, perhaps, but shabby for an Italian'.

Welles' workaholic tendency might well see him live in his clothes. While he was directing *Macbeth* in Harlem in 1936, for example, he worked from 9AM to 6PM, then went into radio rehearsals until midnight, at which point he headed to the cinema to tackle another project. There he took a nap in the projection booth – in his suit – and then rehearsed until dawn. At this point he went for a walk, had a shower, put his suit back on and got back to work. He was just too busy to give much thought to his dress – which made it distinctive.

OSCAR WILDE

1854 – 1900

Oscar Wilde with Lord Alfred Douglas
in 1894 – the relationship that would
cause Wilde's downfall.

'Fashion,' wrote Oscar Wilde, 'is a form of ugliness so intolerable we have to alter it every six months.' 'You can never be overdressed or overeducated,' the writer and playwright would pronounce on another occasion. 'It is only shallow people who do not judge by appearances,' he stated in *The Picture of Dorian Gray*, his novel about a man in pursuit of eternal youth. Wilde, clearly, was never short of a quotable aphorism on the subject of dress.

Certainly Wilde was a recognized stylist of his times, with a flamboyant dress sense that formed just part of his wider appreciation of all things he found beautiful, be they in nature, art or life. He rejected the tailcoats typically worn by men of his times and class – tails have 'no place in costume, except on some Darwinian theory of heredity', he opined. Wilde's loosely tied collars, floral accessories, velvet suits and breeches, cloaks and fur-trimmed overcoats, his hair worn longer than usual for the times (a style captured by society photographer Napoleon Sarony) all made him an easy target for caricaturists. He often appeared in *Punch*, while Gilbert and Sullivan lampooned him in their operetta *Patience*.

Yet, despite this, Wilde had a complex relationship with fashion at large. He was editor of a fashion magazine, *The Woman's World*, but regarded this more an important vehicle for documenting current fashions without necessarily approving of them. ('It seems to me absolutely necessary that [fashion's] growth, development and phases should be duly chronicled … It is quite easy for the children of light to adapt almost any fashionable form of dress to the requirements of utility and the demands of good taste,' he noted in one editorial, entitled 'Slaves of Fashion'). Wilde was also something of a radical activist for change in dress, favouring a more rationalist, 'anti-fashion' approach to it – which appealed to a growing band of artists and intellectuals of the late nineteenth century. He advocated especially change in dress for women, whose painfully corseted strictures of style echoed societally imposed limitations at large. He even went so far as to design looser, more flowing clothes for his wife. 'If one is to behave badly, it is better to be bad in a becoming dress', is a Wilde line presumably not aimed at her.

In one of Wilde's newspaper essays, 'The Philosophy of Dress', for example, he wrote, 'I care nothing at all for frills … but I care a great deal for the wonder and grace of the human form. The beauty of a dress depends entirely and absolutely on the loveliness it shields, and on the freedom and motion that it

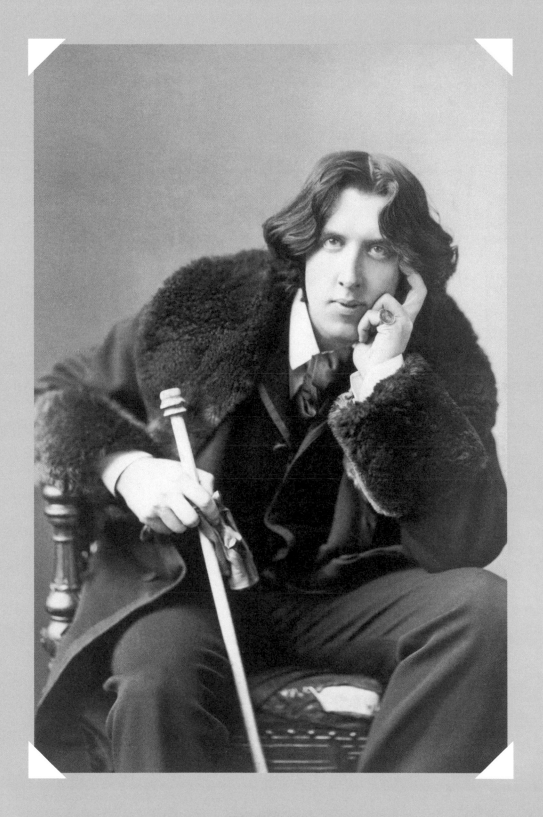

Wilde, photographed by
Napoleon Sarony, ca.1882.

Wilde photograph by Napoleon Sarony in 1882 – his dress was considered eccentric for the times.

Oscar Wilde on holiday in 1893 – his pale attire is artfully punctuated by just two points of colour, his necktie and boutonnière.

'MODERATION IS A FATAL THING. NOTHING SUCCEEDS LIKE EXCESS.'

does not impede.' He predicted – and was not altogether wrong – that during the twentieth century the distinctions of men's and women's dress would fade away, with it emphasizing differences of occupation rather than of gender.

Indeed, Wilde's attitudes and way of life reflected a revolutionary spirit in many ways – one too much so for many. His downfall – imprisonment and hard labour for his illegal homosexuality – saw him leave prison destitute and *persona non grata*. One contemporary account by Frank Harris tells how Wilde begged an intimate of his to get him some clothes. Harris took the name of Wilde's tailor and ordered two suits, but the tailor refused to take the order, such was the aesthete's infamy.

Oscar Wilde in dramatic form, dressed in keeping with the aesthetic movement, in 1882.

OSCAR WILDE

PICTURE CREDITS / ACKNOWLEDGEMENTS

The author and publisher would like to thank the following companies and individuals for permission to reproduce images in this book. In all cases, every effort has been made to credit the copyright holders, but should there be any omissions or errors the publisher would be pleased to insert the appropriate acknowledgement in any subsequent edition of this book.

8 AGIP/Bridgeman Images
9, 10 David Lees/LIFE Picture Collection/Getty Images
11a Gamma-Keystone/Getty Images
11b MARKA/Alamy
12 John Kobal Collection/Moviepix/Getty Images
13, 14a Bettmann/Corbis
14bl GAB Archive/Redferns/Getty Images
14br, 16 LFI/Photoshot
15 John Kobal Collection/Moviepix/Getty Images
17a Bettmann/Corbis
17b Everett Collection/REX Shutterstock
18 Bob Willoughby/Getty Images
19 Graziano Arici/Eyevine
20a Ullstein Bild/Getty Images
20b Photos 12/Alamy
21 Retna/Photoshot
22 UPPA/Photoshot
23 © The Cecil Beaton Studio Archive at Sotheby's
24a John Bulmer/LIFE Picture Collection/Getty Images
24bl Bert Morgan/Getty Images
24br Ullstein Bild/Getty Images
25, 26 Hulton Archive/Getty Images
27, 28ar Bob Thomas Sports Photography/Getty Images
28al PA/TopFoto
28b Tony Sapiano/REX Shutterstock
29 Trinity Mirror/Mirrorpix/Alamy
30 Terry O'Neill/Getty Images
31 Pictorial Press/Alamy
32 Michael Putland/Getty Images
33a Fotos International/Getty Images
33bl Jorgen Angel/Idols/Photoshot
33br Trinity Mirror/Mirrorpix Alamy
34 ITV/REX Shutterstock
35 Jack Robinson/Getty Images
36a Archive Photos/Getty Images
36b Michael Ochs Archive/Getty Images
37 Duffy/Getty Images
38 Hulton Archive/Getty Images

39 Everett Collection/REX Shutterstock
40a Alfred Eisenstadt/The LIFE Picture Collection/Getty Images
40bl FPG/Getty Images
40br Ernest Sisto/New York Times Co/Getty Images
41 Ullstein Bild/Getty Images
42 Pictorial Press/Alamy
43 © 20th Century Fox/Everett/REX Shutterstock
44a Robert Alexander/Getty Images
44b Michael Ochs Archive/Getty Images
45 UPPA/Photoshot
46 Ernest H Mills/ Getty Images
47, 48 Popperfoto/Getty Images
49l Hulton Archive/Getty Images
49r REX Shutterstock
50 Everett Collection/REX Shutterstock
51 Alexander Paal/Condé Nast Collection via Getty Images
52 Eugene Robert Richee/John Kobal Foundation/Getty Images
53ar Bettmann/Corbis
53bl Everett Collection/REX Shutterstock
53br REX Shutterstock
54 Apic/Getty Images
55 Alinari/REX Shutterstock
56a Lebrecht Music and Arts Photo Library/Alamy
56bl Chronicle/Alamy
56br Fondazione Il Vittoriale degli Italiani, Archivio Iconigrafico
57 UPPA/Photoshot
58 Photofest
59, 60 photo Don Hunstein. Courtesy of Sony Music Entertainment
61 Bridgeman Images
62a © Esmond Edwards/CTS Images
62bl Michael Ochs Archive'Getty Images
62br Thierry Trombert/Idols/Photoshotl
63 Anthony Barboza
64 Michael Ochs Archive/Getty Images
65 starstock/Photoshot
66a Disney ABC Television Group/Getty Images
66b, 67 PictureLux/Eyevine
68 Moviestore Collection/REX Shutterstock
69 Dennis Stock/Magnum Photos
70, 71r Moviestore Collection/REX Shutterstock
71l Sunset Boulevard/Corbis
72 Stanley Bielecki Movie Collection/Getty Images

73 François Pages/Paris Match via Getty Images
74l Denis Cameron/REX Shutterstock
74r Paul Popper/Popperfoto/Getty Images
75a Photos 12/Alamy
75b Jean-Pierre Bonnotte/Gamma-Rapho via Getty Images
76, 78a Theo Kingma/REX Shutterstock
77 Carlos Alvarez/Getty Images
78b Rotello/MCP/REX Shutterstock
79 Matt Baron/BEI/REX Shutterstock
80 Illustrated London News/Mary Evans
81 Tavin/Everett/REX Shutterstock
82l, 85a Popperfoto/Getty Images
82r, 84 TopFoto
83 Hirz/Getty Images
85b Reg Burnett/Hulton Royals Collection/Getty Images
86 Hulton Archive/Getty Images
87 Sunset Boulevard/Corbis
88 Moviepix/Getty Images
89l MGM/Kobal
89r Everett Collection/REX Shutterstock
90 Todd Heisler/The New York Times/Redux/Eyevine
91 Walter Iooss Jr/ NBAE/Getty Images
92 Suzanne Vlamis/AP/Press Association
93 Richard Drew/AP/Press Association
94 Reporters Associes/Gamma-Rapho/Getty Images
95 Nicolas Tikhomiroff/Magnum Photos
96ar Guy Le Querrec/Magnum Photos
96br Ulf Andersen/Hulton Archive/Getty Images
96l Gamma-Keystone/Getty Images
97 Daniel Simon/Gamma-Rapho via Getty Images
98 John Engstead/Moviepix/Getty Images
99 Everett Collection/REX Shutterstock
100l & r Everett Collection/REX Shutterstock
101 John Kobal Foundation/Getty Images
102a Silver Screen Collection/Hulton Archive/Getty Images
102b Michael Ochs Archive/Getty Images
103 George Hoyningen-Huene/Condé Nast/Corbis
104 David Redfern/Getty Images
105 David Montgomery/Getty Images
106l Bridgeman Images
106r Warner Bros/The Kobal Collection
107l William James Warren/Science Faction/Corbis
107r REX Shutterstock

108 Express Newspapers/Getty Images
109 © The Cecil Beaton Studio Archive at Sotheby's
110 TopFoto
111a King Collection/Photoshot/Getty Images
111b Donald Maclellan/Getty Images
112 Startraks Photo/REX Shutterstock
113 Hank Walker/The LIFE Collection/Getty Images
114l Paul Schutzer/The LIFE Collection/Getty Images
114r Bridgeman Images
115 Corbis
116 Granamour Weems Collection/Alamy
117 Allen Ginsberg/Corbis
118 Zuma Press, Inc/Alamy
119a Fausto Giaccone/Anzenberger/Eyevine
119b Moviestore Collection/REX Shutterstock
120 Davis/Topical Press Agency/Getty Images
121 courtesy Lacoste
122al Bridgeman Images
122ar Ullstein Bild/Getty Images
122b Sipa Press/REX Shutterstock
123 Underwood & Underwood/Corbis
124 Getty Images for CFDA/Getty Images
125 Contrasto/Eyevine
126 photo Carter Berg courtesy of Ralph Lauren
127 photo Bruce Weber courtesy of Ralph Lauren
128, 130l Peter Mazel/Sunshine/REX Shutterstock
129 Lynn Goldsmith/Corbis
130r Michael Putland/Retna/Photoshot
131 Peter Still/Redferns/Getty Images
132 Collection Christophel/Photoshot
133 Angelo Deligio/Mondadori Portfolio/akg images
134 Giorgio Lotti/Mondadori Portfolio via Getty Images
135l Otfried Schmidt/ullstein bild/Getty Images
135r Graziano Arici/Eyevine
136 Glasshouse Images/REX Shutterstock
137 A F Archive/Alamy
138l Mirisch/Photoshot
138r Moviestore Collection/REX Shutterstock
139l Everett Collection/REX Shutterstock

139r Ullstein Bild/Getty Images
140 Joel Brodsky/Corbis
141 Michael Ochs Archive/Getty Images
142a Tom Copi/Michael Ochs Archives/
Getty Images
142b K & K Ulf Kruger OHG/Redferns/
Getty Images
143 Henry Diltz/Corbis
144 Graziano Arici/Eyevine
145 Terry O'Neill/Iconic Images/
Getty Images
146 Hulton Archive/Getty Images
147l Bradley Smith/Corbis
147r Diltz/RDA/Getty Images
148 Jones/Evening Standard/
Getty Images
149 David Nutter
150 Central Press/Hulton Archive/
Getty Images
151l Trinity Mirror/Mirrorpix/Alamy
151r J & J Crombie Limited
152 AP/Press Association
153 Robert Doisneau/Gamma-Rapho
via Getty Images
154a Paul Popper/Popperfoto/Getty
Images © Succession Picasso/DACS,
London 2016
154b Hulton Archive/Getty Images ©
Succession Picasso/DACS, London 2016
155 Arnold Newman/Getty Images
156 Retna/Photoshot
157 LFI/Photoshot
158al CBS/Getty Images
158ar Globe Photos/REX Shutterstock
158bl Snap/REX Shutterstock
158br Everett Collection/REX Shutterstock
159a Michael Ochs Archive/Getty Images
159b Alfred Wertheimer/Getty Images
160 Terry O'Neill/Getty Images
161 Snap/REX Shutterstock
162l Jonathan Blair/Corbis
162r Warner Bros/The Kobal Collection
163a LFI/Photoshot
163b Silver Screen Collection/
Getty Images
164 Paul Natkin/WireImage/Getty Images
165 Photography by Norman Seeff
166a David Gahr/Getty Images
166bl Richard Young/REX Shutterstock
166br Tony Gale/Pictorial Press/Alamy;167
Graham Wiltshire/Getty Images
168 Everett Collection/REX Shutterstock
169 Photo Edward Quinn ©
edwardquinn.com

170 Ullstein Bild/Getty Images
171l Michael Ochs Archive/Getty Images
171r AP/Press Association
172l Starstock/Photoshot
172r Murray Garrett/Getty Images
173 Gjon Mili/The LIFE Premium
Collection/Getty Images
174 Culture Club/Getty Images
175 Bettmann/Corbis
176 Culture Club/Getty Images
177a Nara Archives/REX Shutterstock
177b Ullstein Bild/Getty Images
178 Picade LLC/Alamy
179 Santi Visalli/Getty Images
180ar Herve Gloaguen/Gamma-Rapho
via Getty Images
180l Picture Alliance/Photoshot © 2016
The Andy Warhol Foundation for the Visual
Arts, Inc/Artists Rights Society (ARS), New
York and DACS, London 2016
180br Starstock/Photoshot
181 The LIFE Picture Collection/
Getty Images
182, 184a, 185r Everett Collection/
REX Shutterstock
183 Moviestore Collection/
REX Shutterstock
184b Michael Ochs Archive/Getty Images
185l Associated Newspapers/
REX Shutterstock
186 Roger-Viollet/Getty Images
187 Library of Congress Prints and
Photographs Division
188l Everett Collection/REX Shutterstock
188r Apic/Getty Images
189 Roger-Viollet/REX Shutterstock.

The author would like to thank
Helen Rochester, Alice Graham, Giulia
Hetherington, Nathan Gale and Davina
Cheung.

Published in 2016 by
Laurence King Publishing Ltd
361–373 City Road
London EC1V 1LR
United Kingdom
Tel: +44 (0)20 7841 6900
Fax: +44 (0)20 7841 6910
e-mail: enquiries@laurenceking.com
www.laurenceking.com

© Text 2016 Josh Sims

Josh Sims has asserted his right
under the Copyright, Designs and
Patents Act 1988, to be identified as
the Author of this Work.

A catalogue record for this book is
available from the British Library

ISBN: 978-1-78067-864-1

Design: Intercity
Picture Research: Giulia Hetherington

Printed in China